Starting in Polymer Clay

To my daughter, Laura, and husband, Luigi, who have patiently put up with objects and projects.

I would like to thank:

My mother, who laid the first stone.
Sonia and Max, who have shared in my first creations.
All those who have been close to me, particularly Gianna.

The Associazione Culturale Scuola d'Arte Leonardo in Prato.
The San Diego Polymer Clay Guild, who collaborated with some of the cane sections included in the introduction.
Pnina, who kindly shared some of the techniques with us.
Paola and Michela Affortunnati, whose creations are presented in this manual, and Giulia.
A special thank you goes to Amelia and Alessandro for their hospitality.

I would like to thank Alberto Bertoldi for his patience, understanding, and professional excellence.
Thanks to Beatrice Brancaccio for her imagination.

A special thank you goes to the following firms:
STAEDTLER ITALIA, who supplied the FIMO material for making some objects.
Cartolibreria R. QUARANTA in Prato.
C.B.M. of C. BAGNOLI & C. of Prato, who collaborated in writing the chapter on materials.

Editor: Cristina Sperandeo
Photography: Alberto Bertoldi
Graphic design and layout: Paola Masera and Beatrice Brancaccio
Translation: Chiara Tarsia

Library of Congress Cataloging-in-Publication Data Available

10 9 8 7 6 5 4 3 2 1

Published in 2003 by Sterling Publishing Co., Inc.
387 Park Avenue South, New York, NY 10016
Originally published in Italy under the title
Modellare con la nuova pasta sintetica.
Also published in the United States under the title
Polymer Clay Basics
©1999 by RCS Libri S.p.A., Milano
English translation ©2000 by Sterling Publishing Co., Inc.
Distributed in Canada by Sterling Publishing
^c/o Canadian Manda Group, One Atlantic Avenue, Suite 105
Toronto, Ontario, Canada M6K 3E7
Distributed in Great Britain by Chrysalis Books
64 Brewery Road, London, N7 9NT England
Distributed in Australia by Capricorn Link (Australia) Pty. Ltd.
P.O. Box 704, Windsor, NSW 2756 Australia

Sterling ISBN 1-4027-0955-2

Starting in Polymer Clay

Techniques, Tools & Projects

Monica Resta

Sterling Publishing Co., Inc.
New York

CONTENTS

INTRODUCTION

In this book you will find all the necessary information to become familiar with heat-hardened polymer clays. I hope it will be a reference to those of you who already know these clays and have fun working with them, and an incentive to those of you who have never used them. A word of warning: this technique is like a Chinese box–once you've opened one, you'll want to open them all. Polymer Clay has been around since the 1930s and were first used for making dolls. They became extremely popular in the 1990s with the spread of the cane technique in the United States. It my mother Mia who first introduced these clays into our home. She "discovered" them in a craft store in the middle of Corso Buenos Aires (Milan), where we lived at the time. My brother Max and I were small and we used to have great fun creating objects and toys. Since 1990, several non-profit cultural associations have sprung up to promote the activities and properties of this clay. The most prominent, or at least the first established, is the National Polymer Clay Guild, which is a source of information, activities, and services for all the hobbyists and artists in the world. Each project presented in this book has a list of materials at the very beginning. The amount of clay indicated is very approximate. Remember that we all cut cane slices differently, so some of the slices will have to be discarded if they are not cut well. In many projects it is possible to correct any mistakes by adding your own personal touch to the result and modifying the original model. I hope this book will be useful to many of you for developing ideas and that it may become a bridge for establishing relations with national and international associations.

BASIC
TECHNIQUES

POLYMER CLAY

Polymer clays are extremely versatile. They are kneaded before they are baked in an oven at a low temperature (from 212°F to 275°F).

They last for many years. Once the object has hardened, it can be filed, cut, and then placed into the oven once again.

If you follow the recommended temperatures, this material does not release toxic gases while baking. Danger of intoxication occurs only when there is combustion.

There are a couple of different brands of polymer clay: Firmo, Cernit, Gemmacolor, Prèmo, Friendly Clay, Modello, Modurit, Limmo, Crealltherm, etc.

Each polymer clay has its own characteristics and the right one must be chosen according to what you are making.

Some are very soft during the kneading phase while others are difficult to soften. The resistance, flexibility, and brightness of the end result will also vary according to the particular brand. The different products can be mixed together without any problems.

These materials are all non-toxic. They are mainly made up of polyvinyl chloride powder, plasticizers, and different types of fill-in substances to give the clay volume. Stabilizers preserve the clay's coloring

characteristics and pigments. PVC, or polyvinyl chloride, is the base of these heat-hardened clays. Polymer clay is made up of one or two molecules of the same compound which, in the presence of a catalyst, becomes united. The chemical uniting process of these molecules, leading to the formation of more complex molecules, is called polymerization. Vinyl chloride (monochlorideethylene) is the gas (Ch2 CHCl) that supplies the polyvinyl chloride (PVC) or vinyl plastic (one of the first plastic materials obtained by synthesis). The polymerization process of the vinyl chloride is highly toxic and only occurs in watertight reactors in large industries. Do not worry! Once it is on the market, PVC powders are non-toxic. Before becoming a clay that can be modeled, other non-toxic compounds must be added to the PVC. It is important that polymer clay has a non-toxic plasticizer, which gives it flexibility, because an irreversible reaction occurs when it is baked. The stabilizer is another compound that hinders thermal deterioration and can have calcium, barium, zinc, etc. as a base.

Last, but not least, fill-in substances are added such as calcium carbonate. Polymer clay is white. Non-toxic color pigments are added to give you an almost endless array of beautiful and vibrant colors.

TOOLS AND PROCEDURES

Working with heat-hardened polymer clay is just like working with normal clay. The only tools you need are those that are commonly found in your home. A good imagination and deft hands are also needed.
Polymer clay is a non-toxic material, but it must be remembered that it is not edible and must, therefore, be kept out of the reach of small children, as they tend to put anything they find into their mouths. As with all artistic products, it is wise not to work near objects that are used to prepare food. Skewers, wire, a grater, and tinfoil will all come in handy. Tinfoil can be used to put your creations on once they are in the oven and to create internal structures in the creations themselves.
Do not forget that certain PVC objects could react if they come in contact with a plasticizer which, as mentioned earlier, is a compound of the clay. To avoid unpleasant surprises and discovering a couple of days later that your clay is stuck to another PVC-based object, it is a good idea to set them apart right from the beginning.
Some clays are harder than others. To soften, leave

the clay on a heater if you are working during the winter months. However, simple manipulation should be enough to soften the clay. If the clay is particularly hard, add a drop or two of oil (any type is fine) and mix it in well. Those of you who have a coffee or meat grinder can soften the clay without any effort and without dirtying your hands.
A smooth, washable top, such as formica or glass, is good to work on. All sorts of dust and dirt particles tend to appear on the clay; make sure, therefore, that your worktable, tools, and hands are always clean.

To spread the clay, use a rolling pin. Using a home pasta machine is an excellent idea, but is not essential. It *is* essential, although, for those of you who are constantly working with polymer clay. To cut well, make sure you have a good craft knife or a sharp razor blade. (Be careful not to cut yourselves!) To obtain identical cane slices, mark the intervals by placing a screw on the cane. The marks on the clay left by the screw will be a guide for cutting. Alcohol is perfect for cleaning your dirty worktable.

I always advise people to sprinkle their hands, tools, and clay objets with some baby powder to prevent them from getting dirty and from sticking. Once the clay is molded and you are satisfied with the result, it is now ready to be baked in the oven. The final treatment of the surface before baking is very important. You can give your work a rough look by dabbing it with a wide-meshed cloth or a smooth look by sprinkling it with some baby powder and delicately rubbing it with your hands.

The clay objects can be placed in the oven on a glass tray.

Once baked, smooth the surface with very thin emery paper. Some clay objects have a bright surface when they come out of the oven. Try polishing them to make them even more brilliant. Alcohol-based enamel is perfect for this. An even simpler and less expensive method is to use a soft, dry cloth and wipe the objects with a neutral-colored shoe polish or bees wax.

Sometimes a little bit of baby powder is left on the objects after they are baked. All you have to do is sprinkle the objects with a drop or two of oil and then dry.

BAKING

If you do not have an oven that you can use exclusively for this type of work, use your kitchen oven. Remember, however, to place the objects in an old pot first because even though polymer clay DOES NOT release toxic gases, they do emanate a rather unpleasant smell. Let the clay objects cool before lifting them out of the pot. Make sure that the objects in the oven do not touch since the heat tends to weld them together.

Polymer clay solidifies only when heated for over 20 minutes at a temperature between 212°F and 266°F. Never cook over 320°F because you risk burning your objects and producing toxic gases. The objects should remain in the oven at a low temperature. Polymer clay maintains a steady temperature for a long time as long as it does not exceed the temperature indicated by the manufacturer. Always follow the instructions printed on the packaging. You can mix different types of polymer clays, but be sure to choose the median temperature of them. When polymer clay solidifies is very important because if the compounds do not fuse well together, the work, although hard, will remain fragile. The minimum time the object should stay in the oven depends on the object's thickness (from 5 to 30 minutes or more). Experiment to find the place in the oven where baking can be carried out in a uniform manner since the heat is not always evenly distributed. A word of warning: some ovens do not stay at the indicated temperature. This is why it is extremely important to try everything out first. Since the baking temperature must be low, wood, cardboard, metals, glass, and ceramics can all be combined with polymer clay. In certain cases it is even possible to add plastic—in this case it is best to use polymer clays that solidify at 212°F. Never use a microwave oven. In these types of ovens, baking occurs from the inside to the outside of the body and the object can explode. Also, keeping track of the temperature is much more difficult than with a normal oven.

COLORS AND PIGMENTS

Polymer clays come in a vast range of colors. It is, however, useful to be able to create different-colored clay colors without having to purchase them. Polymer clay is white. Adding colored-powdered pigments or mixing the neutral-colored clay with acrylic paints will enable you to achieve the color you desire. Paints can be used, but must be quite pasty because polymer clay is water-repellent. Paints, acrylics, and pigments are available from craft stores. The use of color is the most important thing when creating canes.

With a low color contrast, the shapes will appear drab and their details will get lost as the pattern gradually gets smaller.

Contrast can be obtained through the use of a few tricks: (1) the chiaroscuro technique, which is a play of luminosity between adjacent areas; (2) combining warm and cool colors together; and (3) combining soft and intense colors together.

Warm colors are those that go from purple-red to yellow while the cool ones range from yellow-green to purple on the chromatic wheel. In the chromatic

spectrum, the warm colors are opposite the cool ones.

Beginners are advised to use monochromatic colors (belonging to a single range) or primary colors, which, when mixed together, create secondary colors.

For example, using yellow, blue, and white, you will obtain a light green. I recommend that you do not combine complementary colors because they could produce a neutral color when mixed together, which is not always pleasing to the eye.

The primary colors are:

RED – YELLOW – BLUE: They cannot be obtained by mixing with other colors. These colors cannot be broken down. Secondary colors, on the other hand, can be obtained by mixing two primary colors:

RED + YELLOW = ORANGE
BLUE + YELLOW = GREEN
RED + BLUE = PURPLE

BLACK and WHITE are not chromatic colors, but exist as pigments.

RED and GREEN, ORANGE and BLUE, PURPLE and YELLOW are complementary colors. They have no colors in common. As well as pigments, other elements, which do not lose their properties once combined, can be mixed into polymer clay. These are: gold leaf, silver leaf, glitter, pepper, chili, and clay powders.

To create a granite-like effect, mix white clay, glitter, and black pepper. These products are all available in craft stores as well as in supermarkets.

THE CANE TECHNIQUE

CANES

The cane technique enables polymer clay to be modeled like a kaleidoscope: endless colored shapes succeed one another. This technique dates back to the Egyptians (4,000 BC) and became popular with the Venetians in the 15th century. Today, in Murano, Venice, beautiful objects are still being made with this technique. The cane technique can also be applied to other materials, such as wax.

With this technique it is possible to create a three-dimensional image by using colored polymer clay. By creating various sections that are parallel to each other in a common direction, it is possible to achieve a series of two-dimensional images similar to each other that depict the first created shape.

Don't worry: it's simple!

Let's take a cinnamon bun as an example: Think of a layer of soft dough for desserts and a layer of chocolate cream. When you roll them up and then cut the bun into slices, every slice will have the same curled pattern.

This same principle holds for the cane technique.

From these canes, numerous slices can be cut, and each piece will have the same image.

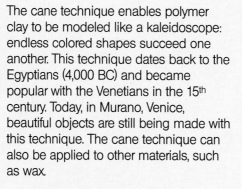

What can be done with all these shapes? You can decorate necklaces, boxes, frames, bottles, pencils, and many other objects. The slices are applied to the surface of the object to be decorated. Polymer clay tends to adhere easily to any kind of structure, so there is no risk of it falling off during the working phases. Also, since the clay remains soft for a long period of time, you can resume your work at any time. What is particularly fascinating about this technique is that the original image can be reduced by simply elongating or thinning out the parallelepiped or cylinder. The pattern inside will always be the initial one, only smaller. I will explain how to create these different patterns by beginning with the simpler ones, for example the dot, and then proceeding to the more difficult ones, like faces.

Canes do not necessarily have to be worked on in the same day. You can store them for long periods of time in plastic bags and then reuse them for other projects.

MAIN SHAPES

To create canes, you need to be familiar with three geometric solids: cylinder, parallelepiped, and prism. These will be used as pieces for creating the pattern. The motif will be a three-dimensional puzzle.

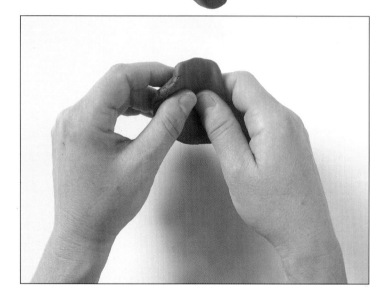

To make a sheet of clay, soften some polymer clay, kneading it with your hands. Then spread it out on your worktable with a rolling pin. Place skewers on either side of the clay so that the thickness is uniform all over.

Cut the edges to obtain a rectangular or square sheet of clay, according to your needs.

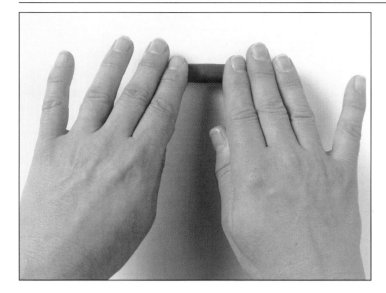

To make a cylinder, roll some clay onto your worktable.
Trim both ends.

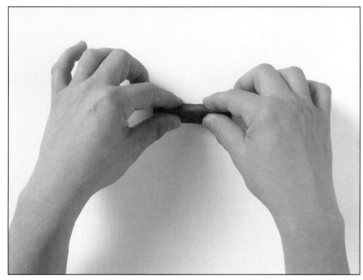

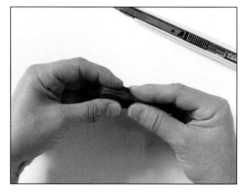

To make a prism, roll some clay into a "sausage". Press it on your worktable in order to create one of the sides. Mold the top with your fingers, thinning the clay along the top part, thus forming the other two sides. Cut the ends to have a perfect prism.

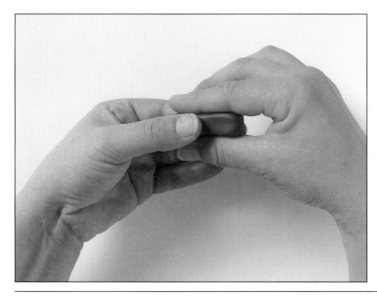

To make a parallelepiped, hold a cylinder between your index fingers and thumbs. Mold the opposite sides with each hand. Finish off the shape using your worktable as a support. Trim the ends and your parallelepiped is ready.

DOTS

The act of elongating and rolling polymer clay is very easy.

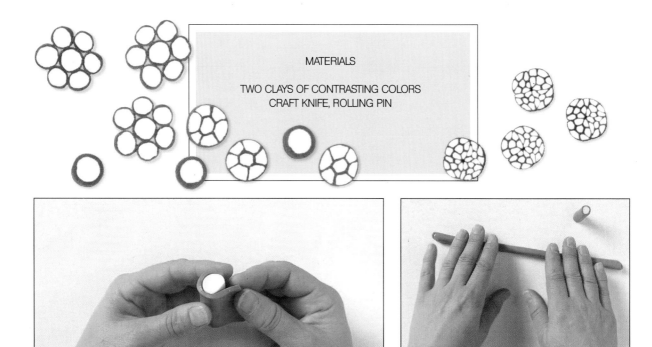

MATERIALS

TWO CLAYS OF CONTRASTING COLORS
CRAFT KNIFE, ROLLING PIN

Roll the clay into a thin log. Choose a different colored clay and roll it out into a sheet. Roll this new cylinder lengthwise. Its center will be a dot.

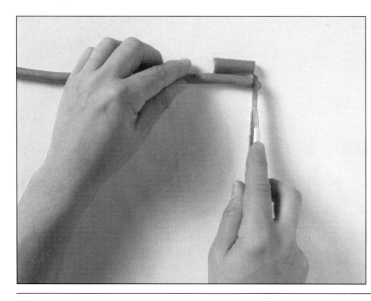

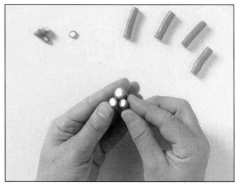

Elongate the log and then cut it up into various segments (7 segments were cut for this project). Use one of these segments as the center of your pattern. Distribute the others around it.

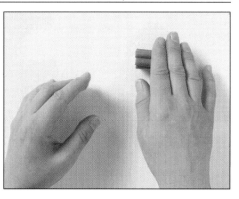

You will now have obtained your first pattern, which should be similar to the one shown in the photo. This new cylinder can be rolled and streamlined.

Divide this new cane into four segments and arrange them next to each other. Unite them. Having obtained a new motif (a bee's nest), you will now be able to make a parallelepiped. From this shape, rectangular or square layers can be made that can decorate frames, boxes, shells, etc.

A cylinder is the best geometric shape to cover spherical surfaces, such as beads. With the craft knife, cut some thin slices. From this pattern you will be able to obtain different shapes.

STRIPES

Canes can take on different geometric shapes. Regular shaped canes make the squeezing process easier. When making canes with a striped motif, a parallelepiped is the geometric shape we need. This pattern is one of the simplest to make, as all you need to do is overlap equal layers of different colored clays.

MATERIALS

DIFFERENT COLORED CLAYS,
CRAFT KNIFE, ROLLING PIN

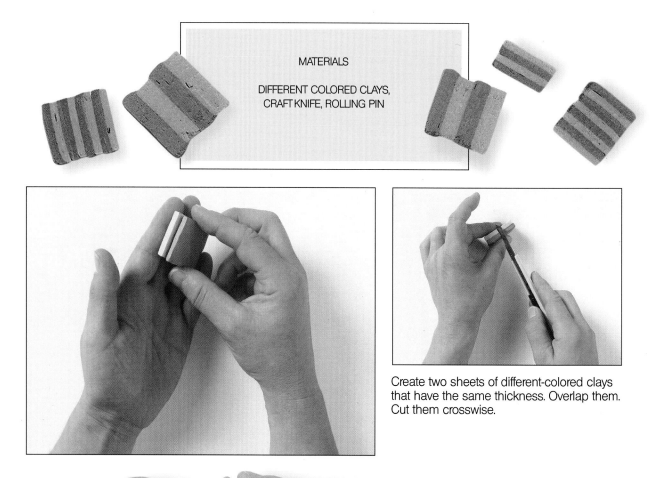

Create two sheets of different-colored clays that have the same thickness. Overlap them. Cut them crosswise.

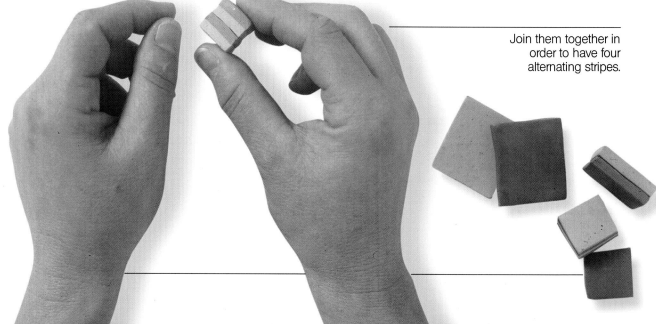

Join them together in order to have four alternating stripes.

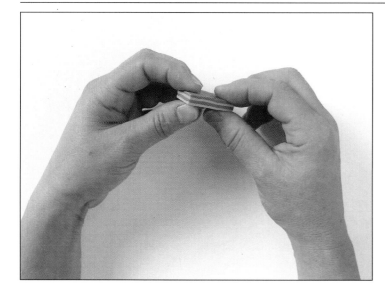

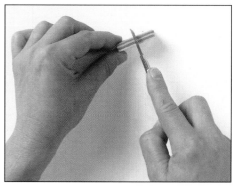

Squeeze the parallelepiped by slightly pressing along its surface. With your hands, make a squeezing and elongating movement.
Patience is required when carrying out this step.

Divide the shape into various slices with a craft knife in order to have a new series of overlapping stripes. In this way you will have obtained a parallelepiped in which every single slice will be like a series of stripes, as already seen in the previous project.

CHESSBOARD

The previous project described how to make stripes. Making squares is the next step up. To make squares easily, we recommend you work with stripes that are about ⅛-inch thick.

MATERIALS

TWO DIFFERENT COLORED CLAYS,
CRAFT KNIFE, ROLLING PIN

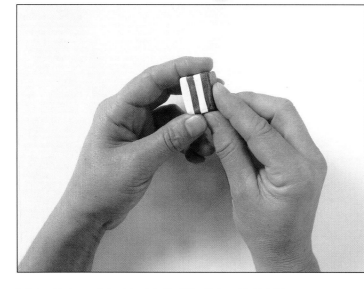

Overlap the stripes (at least four or another even number). Cut the parallelepiped into slices that are the same thickness as the height of the stripes (⅛ inch).

Turn over and place the sections in an alternate manner. Begin with a dark square, then with a white one. Place the slices next to each other and join them together. You will have made a parallelepiped with the first chessboard.

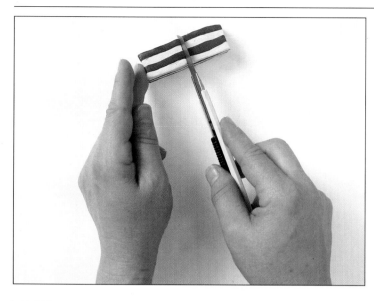

The previous chessboard can be lengthened by slightly pressing the sides of the parallelepiped. Cut in half. You will now have two smaller chessboards. Join them so that the dark squares are next to the white squares.

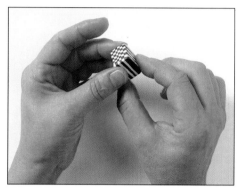

This parallelepiped can be elongated even further in order to obtain an even smaller chessboard. Remember, however, that the ends of the cane must always be discarded because they are always uneven.

A coffee cup is decorated with chessboard squares.

Here are slices of different dimensions.

INTERWEAVING

This decoration gives excellent results. Always make sure, however, that the colors you use strongly contrast with one another and that the darker color is the one that encloses the lighter color. This will give the optical illusion of full-fledged interweaving.

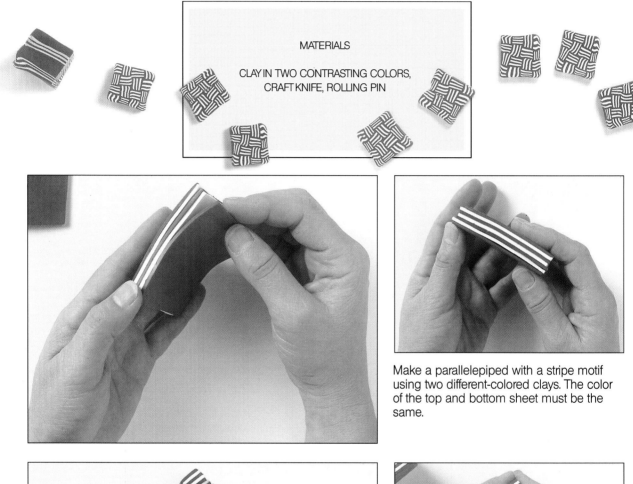

MATERIALS

CLAY IN TWO CONTRASTING COLORS, CRAFT KNIFE, ROLLING PIN

Make a parallelepiped with a stripe motif using two different-colored clays. The color of the top and bottom sheet must be the same.

Cut the parallelepiped into four parts and arrange them by alternating the vertical stripes with the horizontal ones. You will now have completed the first step.

Streamline the parallelepiped by squeezing and elongating each side. Cut the shape in half. Join together, alternating the vertical stripes with the horizontal ones.

As with the previous parallelepiped, elongate it carefully. Cut it in half once more. You will have made two identical canes.

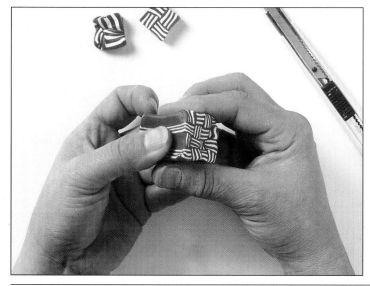

Make the horizontal stripes coincide with the vertical ones and elongate the new cane. Divide the parallelepiped and you have an example of interweaving.

TWIRLS

How many times have you eaten a cinnamon bun? Each slice is made up of a twirl.
The cinnamon bun in this project, however, cannot be eaten, but it can be used to make tons of creations!

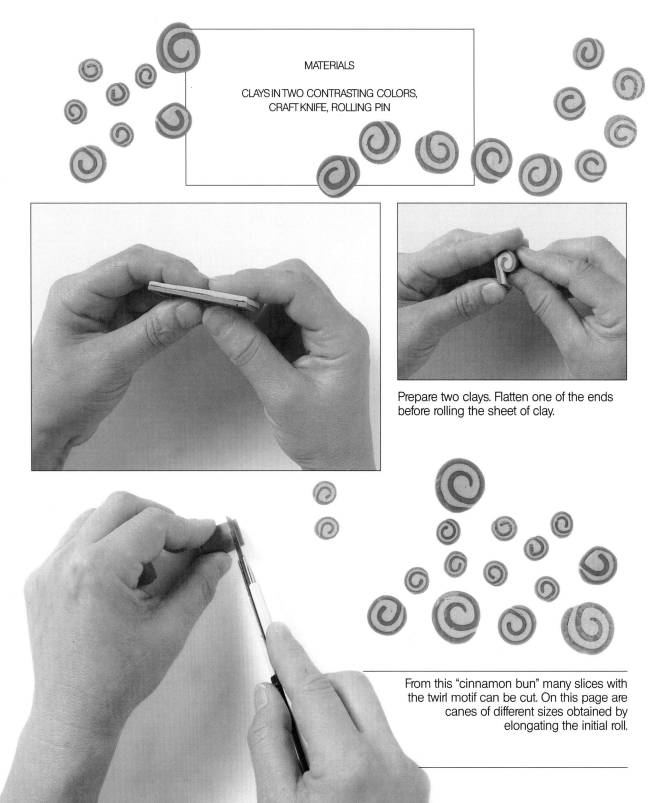

MATERIALS

CLAYS IN TWO CONTRASTING COLORS,
CRAFT KNIFE, ROLLING PIN

Prepare two clays. Flatten one of the ends before rolling the sheet of clay.

From this "cinnamon bun" many slices with the twirl motif can be cut. On this page are canes of different sizes obtained by elongating the initial roll.

THE HERRINGBONE PATTERN

The herringbone pattern, like the chessboard, is made with stripes.
With the herringbone, as with many geometric shapes,
it is possible to make countless other shapes.

MATERIALS

CLAY IN TWO CONTRASTING COLORS,
CRAFT KNIFE, ROLLING PIN

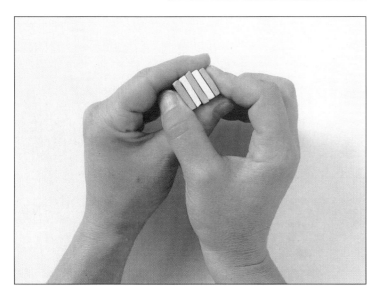

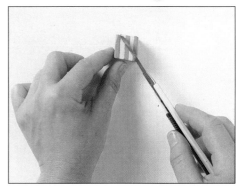

Make a series of clay sheets with two different colors. Overlap them, alternating the colors. The same color must be on the top and on the bottom of the main body. Cut diagonally.

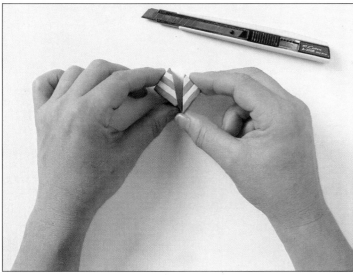

Rotate one of the prisms so that the stripes of the two shapes coincide. Join the two prisms together. The stripes will be aligned and form a herringbone. Slice the parallelepiped. To get smaller images of the same pattern, elongate the parallelepiped.

AN ETHNIC NECKLACE

Black and white are colors which, because of their contrast, are suitable for making motifs that are visible even from a distance. This necklace will be seen and appreciated. Remember that to make canes, very little clay is needed. The necklace in this project requires two different baking times. The first baking time is when the 21 or 22 beads, making up the necklace, have been made. The second is when the whole necklace has been strung and a last bead, which hides the closing knot of the necklace, needs to be baked. Follow the instructions for making these beads. After you have made holes in them, one at a time, stick a skewer through them. Bake for about 30 minutes at 266°F.

With some black and white clay, create some canes with the following motifs:
Stripes: overlap layers of black and white clay over each other.

MATERIALS

FOR THE NECKLACE: WHITE CLAY (2 OZ.), BLACK CLAY (2 OZ.), 4 YD. OF WHITE TWINE, 4 IN. OF THIN WIRE
FOR THE EARRINGS: WHITE AND BLACK CLAY (2 OZ.), TWO NAILS, TWO HOOKS
FOR THE BRACELET: BLACK CLAY (1 OZ.), WHITE CLAY (1 OZ.), BRACELET STRUCTURE, CRAFT KNIFE, BAKING EQUIPMENT

---

of white rolls coated in black clay.
Herringbone: cut a parallelepiped with the stripe motif on the diagonal part of its smaller side. Rotate forward one of the two prisms so that its opposite side is turned upside down.

BRACELET:
Black and white interweaving can be the motif for creating a bracelet that matches the necklace and earrings. The structure was bought from a trinket shop.

BLACK AND WHITE EARRINGS:
This ethnic necklace may be worn with a pair of earrings similar to those for this project.

Twirl: place one sheet of black clay over a white one. Roll, making sure the black clay remains on the outside.
Interweaving: alternate parallelepipedes with a series of horizontal and vertical stripes (starting and ending with black).
Bee's nest: join a series

MAKING BEADS

For the central bead: cut the herringbone cane into four sections (each section must be about ⅛-inch thick). Join the pieces together and create a design made up of concentric squares.

To make two beads with the interweaving pattern, make a small cylinder with some black clay. Cover its perimeter with a sheet of clay taken from the cane with the interweaving motif. With your index finger, round the top and bottom part of the cylinder.

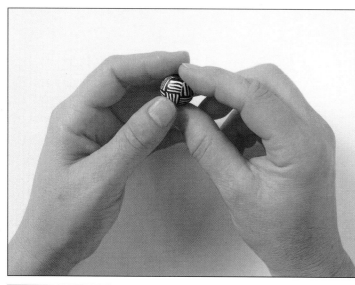

You will need a little patience, but in the end you will have a bead with the chosen motif. To make two round beads with the stripe motif, follow the same instructions for the interlacing, using stripes instead.

To make elongated beads (either straight or twisted), make four rolls and place a thin layer of clay with the stripe motif over them. Round the ends of each cylinder.

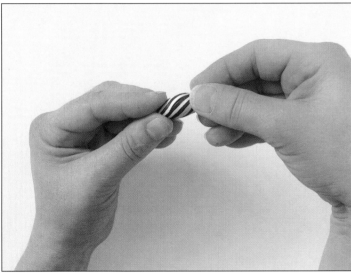

Twist each end in opposite directions with two of the four beads with the stripe motif. To make two beads with the twirl, apply some slices with the twirl motif to a bead. Smooth the beads in the palm of your hands.

Do the same with the bee's nest. Make two black beads and four completely white ones. Once you have made 21 beads, stick a skewer into them and place them into the oven. Make sure that the holes in the beads are big enough to be strung onto the piece of twine. Bake for about 30 minutes at about 266°F.

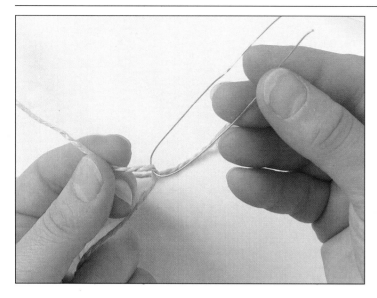

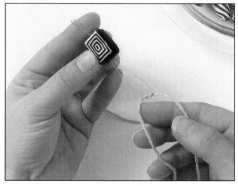

HOW TO ASSEMBLE THE NECKLACE

Take a piece of twine (about three times the length of the finished necklace) and, using a hairpin like a needle, start stringing the beads.

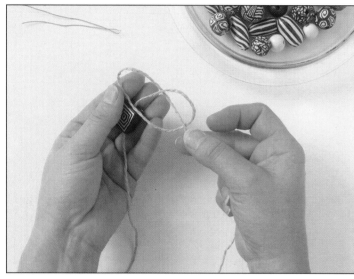

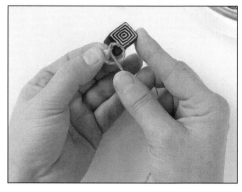

First string the central bead with the concentric squares. Once strung on, tie a knot on either side of the bead.

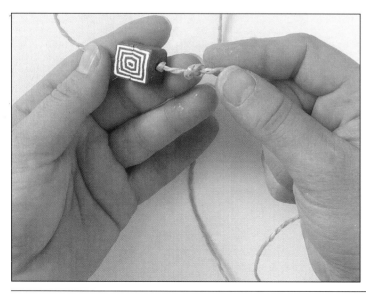

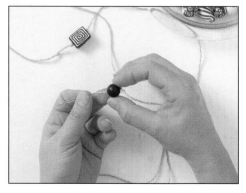

Tie another knot at a distance of about 1¼ inches on either side of the piece of twine. String the black beads, one per side.

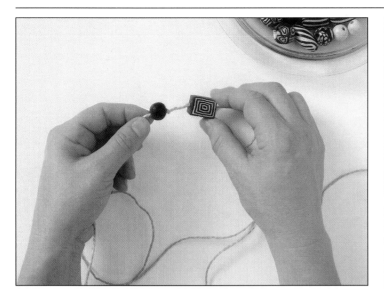

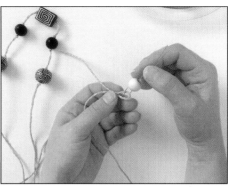

Continue to string the beads, always tying a knot before and after each one has been strung on. Once all the 21 beads are in their places, join the ends of the necklace. Leave enough space between the knot and the last beads to string.

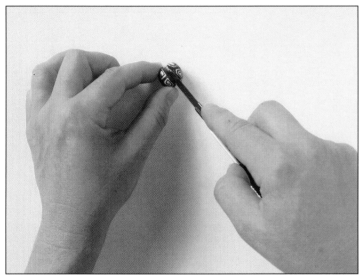

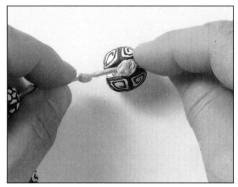

With some black clay, make a bead and then coat it with some cane slices with the twirl motif. Now make a transversal cut. Insert the last joining knot of the necklace into the bead you have just cut.

With a little bit of pressure, close the bead so that the knot is no longer visible. Place the necklace into the oven and bake for another 20 minutes. The twine, even if it is made partly of a synthetic material, will not be damaged in the oven.

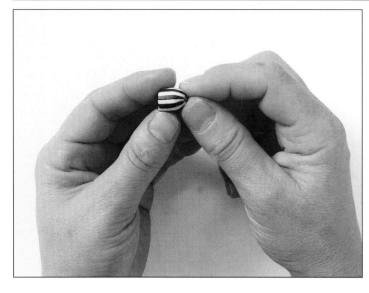

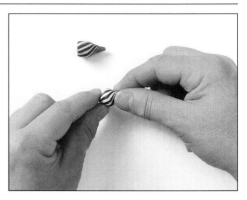

EARRINGS

Make an even cylinder with the black clay. Coat it with a series of cane slices with the stripe motif. Streamline one of the ends to give it the shape of a drop. Twist it.

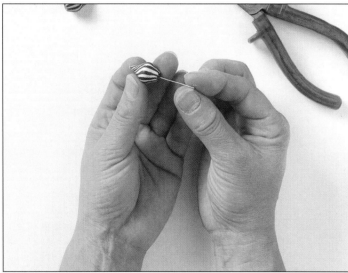

Using thin nails, piece the earrings. Bake for about 30 minutes at 266°F. Once baked, pass the nails into the holes. With a pair of pliers bend the top part of the nail.

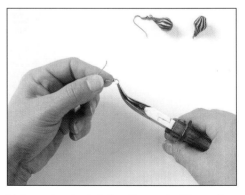

Make a ring by twisting the end of the nail. Open the eyelets of the earrings.

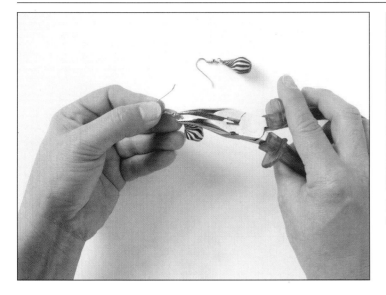

Lastly, insert the earrings and close the eyelets.

BRACELET

Apply cane slices with the interlacing motif onto the base of the bracelet. Slightly press so that they adhere well between each other and the base of the bracelet. Do the same on the inside.

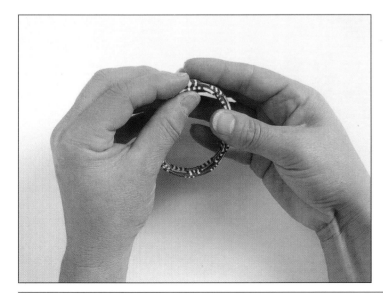

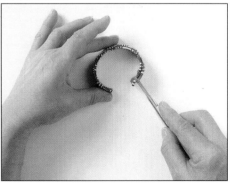

Join the side edges. Remove any excess clay, making sure that the top coating of the bracelet remains attached to the bottom part. Place the bracelet into the oven and bake for 30 minutes at 266°F.

THE SUN

The main elements for making the sun are the cylinder and the plane. The perpendicular projection of a cylinder on a plane is the circumference (the center of the sun) while for a plane it is the stripe (the rays of the sun).

MATERIALS

YELLOW CLAY, RED CLAY, BLUE CLAY,
CRAFT KNIFE, ROLLING PIN

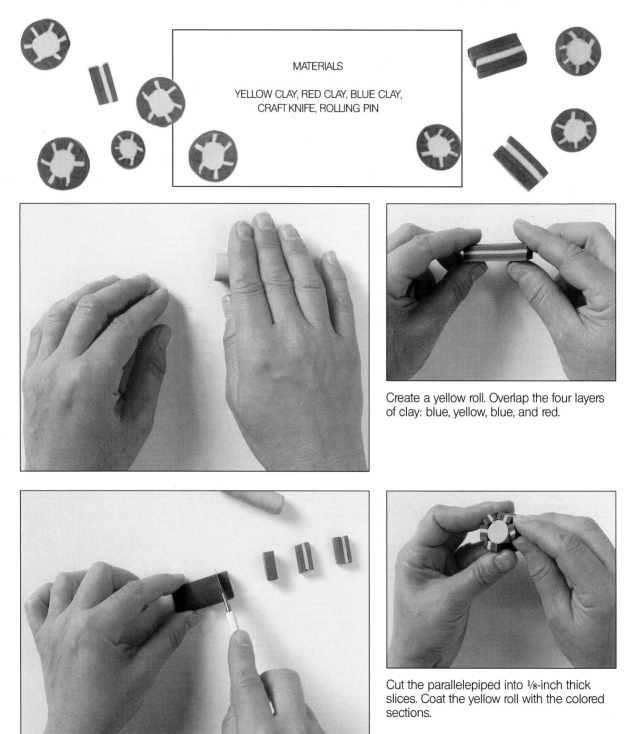

Create a yellow roll. Overlap the four layers of clay: blue, yellow, blue, and red.

Cut the parallelepiped into ⅛-inch thick slices. Coat the yellow roll with the colored sections.

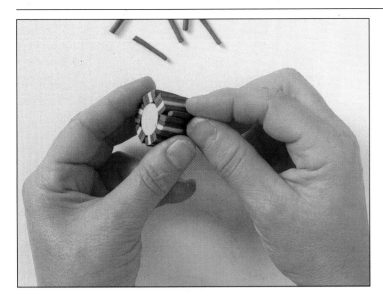

Some gaps will inevitably form around the perimeter while you are arranging the colored slices. Fill them in by inserting small rolls of blue clay. With a layer of blue clay, coat the new cylinder.

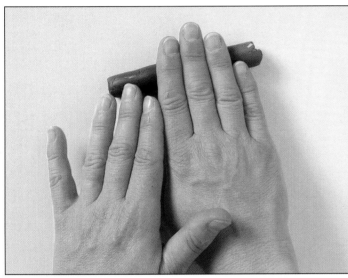

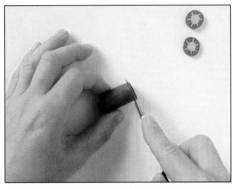

Slowly and evenly elongate the log. Remove the ends of the cane (the pattern is deformed laterally), and then cut it to have many similar images of the sun.

These slices of cane can be applied, along with other canes with the heart or the stripe motif, onto the bracelet. Put the bracelet into the oven and bake for 30 minutes at 266°F.

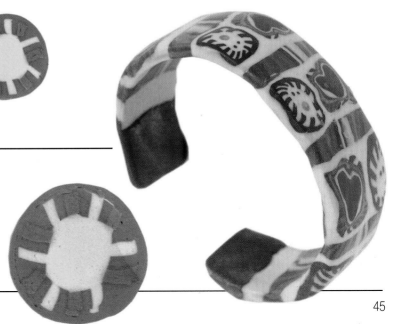

HEARTS

This project uses cylinders, portions of cylinders, prisms, and planes. To give greater contrast to the heart against the green background, outline it in light pink. After having created the motif, fill it in sideways to enclose it in a circle. This way you will have a cylinder that can easily be reduced.

MATERIALS

RED CLAY, PINK CLAY,
GREEN CLAY, CRAFT KNIFE

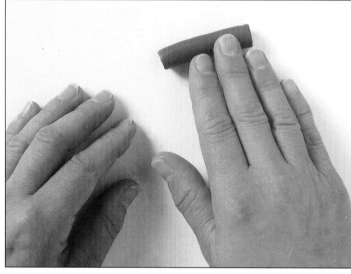

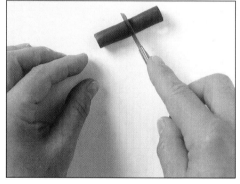

Make a cylinder using red clay. Cut in half. The two rolls will be the top part of the heart.

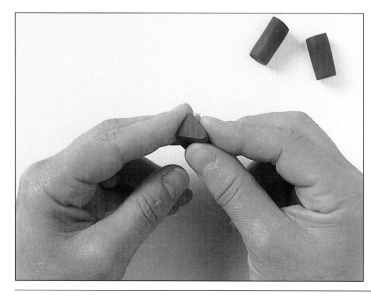

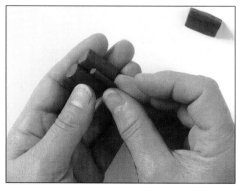

With some more red clay, make a prism, which will be the bottom part of the shape. Make a very thin roll of red clay and use it to fill in the empty spaces between the two top cylinders of the heart.

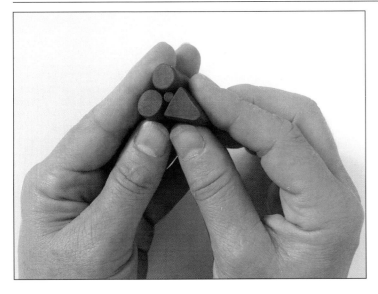

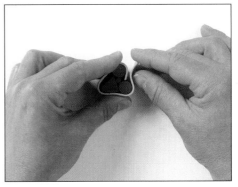

To the three "sausages" (two big ones and one small one), attach the prism as shown in the photo. Create a layer of pink clay to outline this first heart.

With some green clay, make three parts of a cylinder and a small, thin cord. The cord will be used to fill in the top part of the heart, the sections of the cylinder, the sides, and the top part. Join them together.

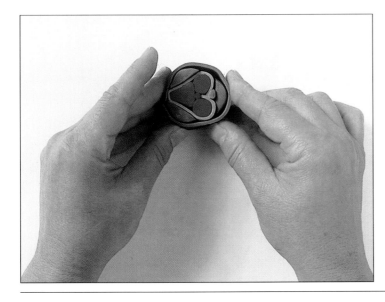

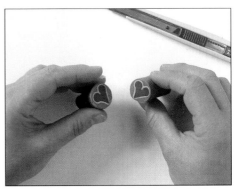

Apply a sheet of green clay. Mold the cylinder and cut.

STARS

Colorful stars illuminate an intense blue sky. Whether they are real or not, these stars will not tire the eyes of the beholder. Small, medium, or big, they can be used to decorate thousands of objects. We will use three geometrical shapes for making our design: the plane, cylinder, and prism.

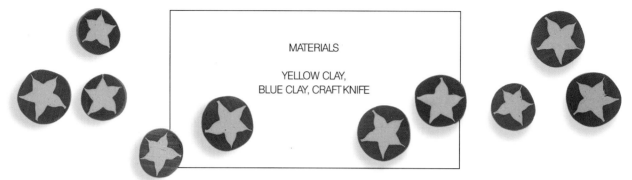

MATERIALS

YELLOW CLAY,
BLUE CLAY, CRAFT KNIFE

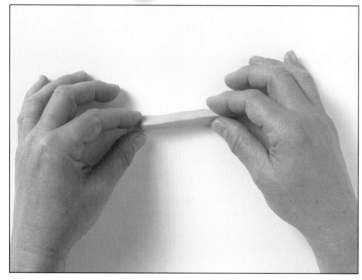

Make a long prism with some yellow clay. The section must be an isosceles triangle (the equal sides are greater than the base). Divide into four equal parts.

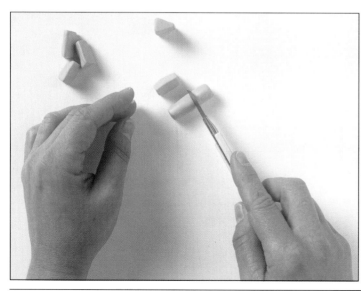

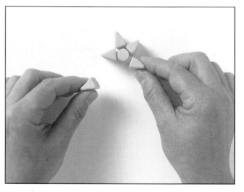

Using yellow clay, make a cylinder that is the same height as the five prisms. With the roll in the center and the prisms around it, join the shapes together.

Make five blue isosceles prisms. This time the base must be greater than the two equal sides. The blue prisms will fill in the space between the tips of the stars.

Apply a layer of blue clay around the entire shape. Slightly squeeze the pattern with your hands, giving it a cylindrical form. Slightly and evenly press on the perimeter and elongate the cylinder.

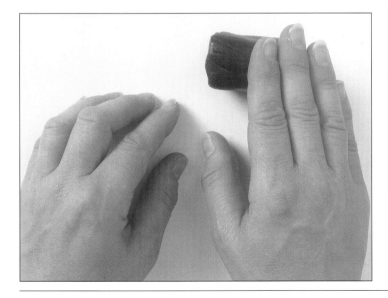

Continue to roll the cylinder on your worktable. Throw away the ends of the cane. The more you elongate the cylinder, the smaller the pattern will become.

FLOWERS

Flowers can have four, five, or more petals. In this example, I chose to make five petals. It is possible to create flowers of different colors. Always keep in mind, however, that the color contrast is very important. Remember that it is possible to obtain a good result even with very little bit of clay.

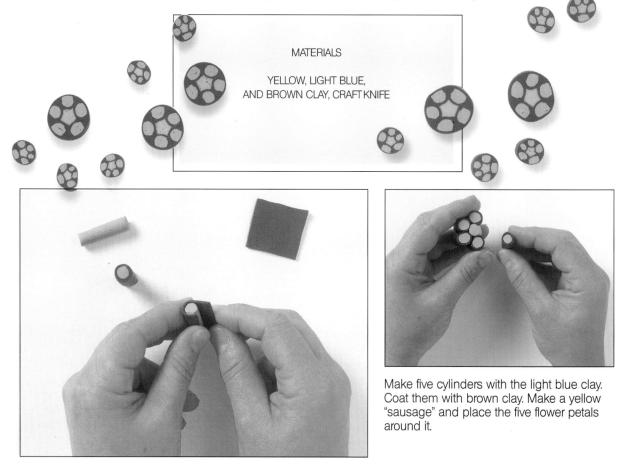

MATERIALS

YELLOW, LIGHT BLUE, AND BROWN CLAY, CRAFT KNIFE

Make five cylinders with the light blue clay. Coat them with brown clay. Make a yellow "sausage" and place the five flower petals around it.

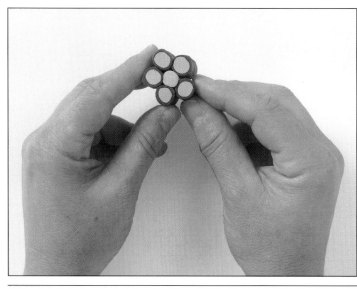

Insert a thin, brown log in-between each petal.

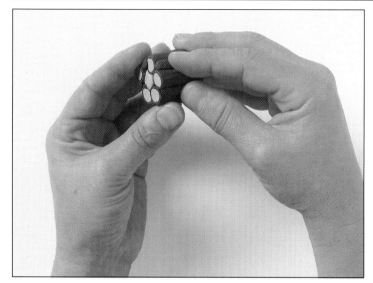

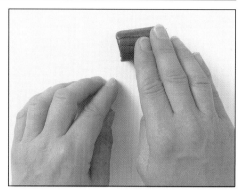

Elongate the cylinder with your hands. Continue to elongate it by rolling the cylinder on your worktable.

It is possible to make canes of different sizes. By cutting this log, you will have in every slice a flower that is very similar to the previous one.

COFFEE CUPS

Simple shapes, such as squares and flowers, are used as decorations for this project. Once completed, the objects are placed into the oven. The baking time must be followed; otherwise, the clay objects will turn out uncooked. Do not exceed the temperature indicated by the clay manufacturer and put the objects into a preheated oven. If the instructions are followed, then 30 minutes in the oven is enough time to obtain a good result. Cups and other types of objects can be washed in lukewarm water. Do not use a dishwasher.

MATERIALS

BLUE CLAY (1½ OZ.), WHITE CLAY (1½ OZ.), YELLOW CLAY (⅛ OZ.), TWO WHITE COFFEE CUPS, TWO SAUCERS, A SUGAR BOWL, TWO COFFEE SPOONS, A CREAMER, CRAFT KNIFE, ROLLING PIN, BAKING EQUIPMENT

The lid of the sugar bowl was decorated with different types of decorations on its surface.
The creamer was decorated in the same way as the cups: with squares "sandwiched" in-between two rows of flowers while the handle was covered in blue with four flowers decorating both ends.
To decorate the teaspoons, follow the instructions in the chapter about decorating flatware.
The motif used to decorate the cups was made up of white squares and squares with the twirl motif.

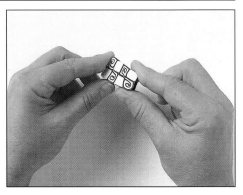

Using blue and white clay, create some canes with the twirl motif. Place next to them a white parallelepiped with the same dimensions. In this way you will create the pattern to make the squares. Join together two patterns, alternating the white squares with those with the twirl motif.

Give the remaining log the shape of a trapezoid. Squeeze a short side of the trapezoid so that it follows the curve at the base of the cup. Cut many thin slices. Apply them onto the cup so that the white squares are next to those with the twirl motif.

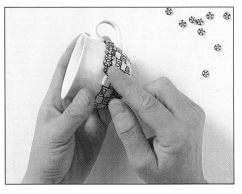

Lastly, create a cylinder with a flower motif. Cut the amount of slices necessary to cover the top part of the decoration. Every slice must be arranged so that a strip overlaps the decoration.

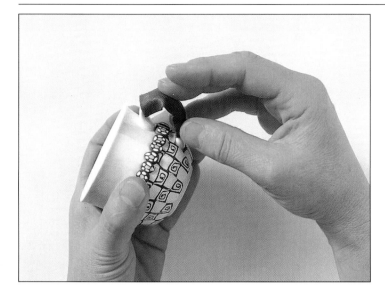

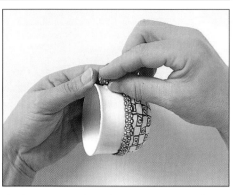

To decorate the handle, apply a layer of blue clay. Add three canes to the two ends of the handle.

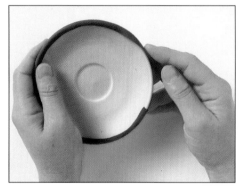

The cup is now completed and you can place it into the oven to bake. The saucer was decorated only around the edge. Make a thin layer of blue clay and arrange it around the rim of the saucer.

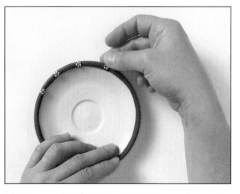

Make sure it adheres well to the surface of the saucer. With a craft knife, eliminate any excess clay. Decorate the rim of the saucer with some flowers. Once decorated, place it into the oven. Turn off the oven and let it cool.

THE MOON

This project will show you how to make a smiling half moon, which you can use with the stars. You will use prisms and cylinders to make it.

MATERIALS

BLACK AND YELLOW CLAY,
CRAFT KNIFE

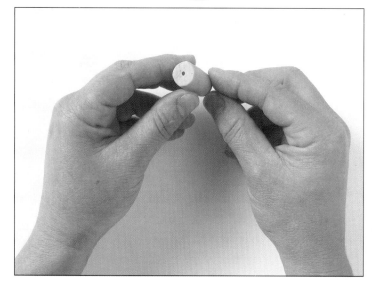

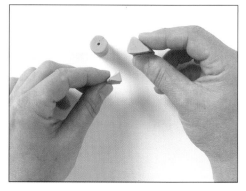

With some black clay, make a small "sausage." Roll some light yellow clay around it to make the moon's eye. With some more clay of the same color, make two isosceles prisms with different dimensions.

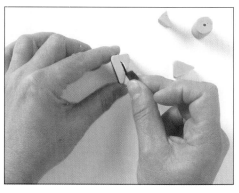

Make a third isosceles prism, but this time a little bit bigger. With a craft knife, cut the prism sideways. Insert into the cut a thin strip of red clay.

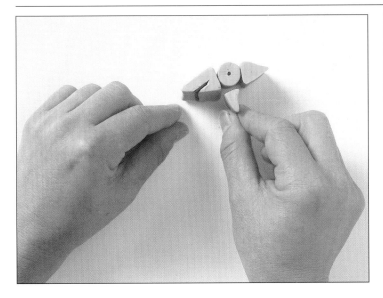

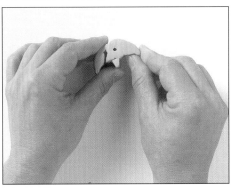

Arrange the geometric shapes as shown in the photo. Join them together. With your hands, mold the parts together, giving them the shape of a moon.

Make lots of black strips that are as long as the depth of the moon. Insert as many "sausages" as necessary to fill in the moon within the cylinder. Apply a layer of black clay around the design.

Start elongating the cane with your hands. Continue lengthening the cane by rolling the cylinder on your worktable. In this way you will obtain canes with different diameters.

DAISIES

The technique, used to make daisies, resembles images in a kaleidoscope.
A section of a daisy is made first, which is then repeated until the motif is complete. This technique may be used to create regular shapes.

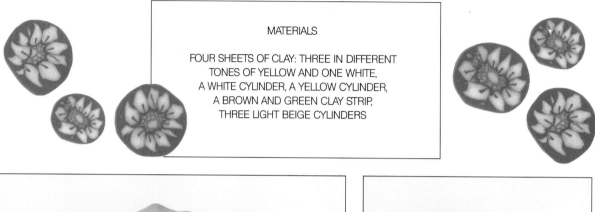

MATERIALS

FOUR SHEETS OF CLAY: THREE IN DIFFERENT
TONES OF YELLOW AND ONE WHITE,
A WHITE CYLINDER, A YELLOW CYLINDER,
A BROWN AND GREEN CLAY STRIP,
THREE LIGHT BEIGE CYLINDERS

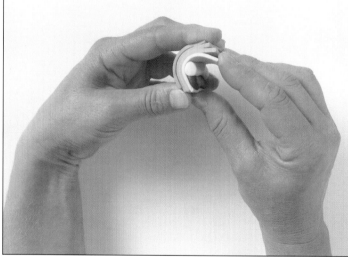

From the darkest color to the lightest, overlap the clay sheets. Bend the sheets into an arch-like shape, leaving the darker color on the outside. Insert, inside the arch, first the white cylinder and then the brown strip. Close the arch and join the whole work.

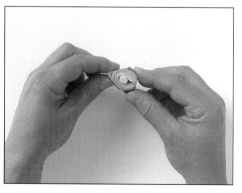

Apply a strip of green clay on the lower sides. Streamline the top part.

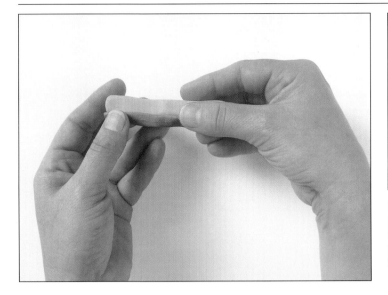

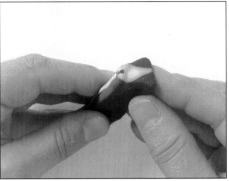

Elongate and squeeze the motif. On the top part insert, on each side, prisms made with the brown clay. The shape of the assembled pieces should look like a prism cut at the top.

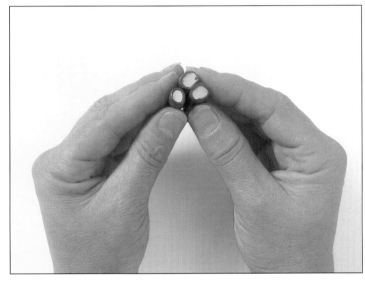

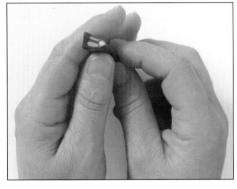

Make three small cylinders with the light beige. Apply a brown sheet of clay. Join them together with two cylinders acting as the base, and one at the top as shown in the photo. Elongate and streamline the shape. Give the whole object the shape of a triangular prism.

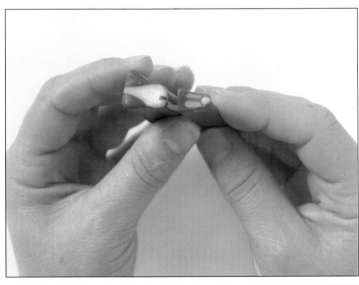

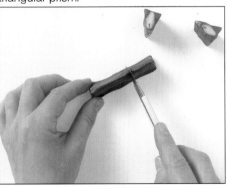

Stick it to the previously made pattern. Cut it into six vertical sections.

Arrange the sections into a fan, giving them the shape of a half cylinder. In the central part, insert half of a yellow cylinder.

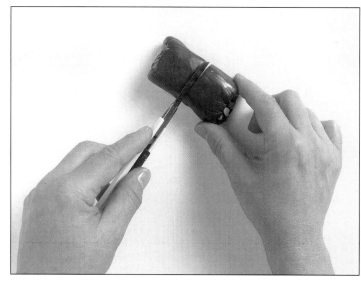

Elongate this new shape and make a cut down the center. Arrange the sections into a mirror-like effect.

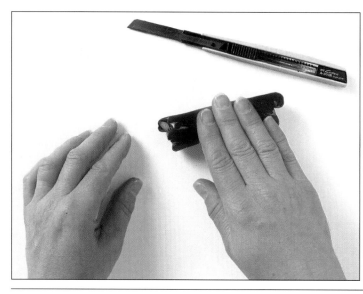

Roll and elongate. Cut the ends of the cylinder until you have a complete image of the daisy. You may streamline the cylinder further in order to have even smaller cylinders.

TULIPS

To create an image with the cane technique, try to break up the figure into geometrical shapes. For example, a tulip may be divided into a semicircle, two triangles, 2 rhombi, and a line.
In a three-dimensional perspective, these shapes become a cylinder divided in half, a triangular prism, a rhomboid, a parallelepiped, and a plane.

MATERIALS

BLUE CLAY, WHITE CLAY,
CRAFT KNIFE

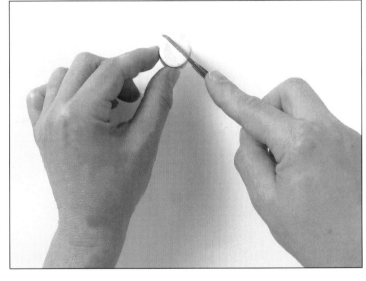

Mold a cylinder with the white clay. Cut it in half. Divide one of the remaining portions into two equal parts.

Flatten the curved side of the shapes. Place the two prisms onto the cut side of the cylinder. Make the stem by inserting a layer of white clay between two of the blue. The resulting parallelepiped should be placed in the middle of the flower's lower part.

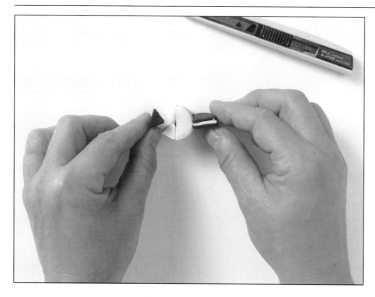

Make a blue-colored prism and insert it between the two white ones.
To form the flower leaves, make two white logs and cover them with a blue layer.

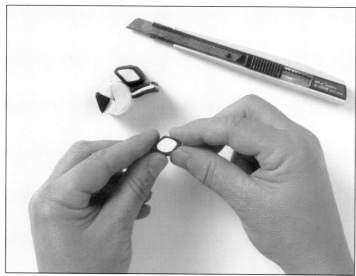

Give them an oval shape and position them at the two sides of the stem.
Insert small blue sticks to fill in the empty spaces between the leaves and the flower.

The flower is already becoming visible.
Add some blue colored clay around the flower, giving the composition a cylindrical shape.

Apply a blue strip to the entire object. Begin delicately thinning the center with your hands.

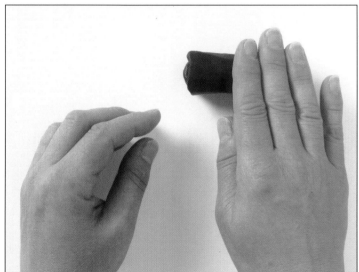

Continue lengthening by placing the cane on your worktable and rolling it with your hands.
After you cut the two ends of the cylinder, you will have a tulip.

This frame was created by applying the canes with the tulip design. A layer of blue clay was spread over the frame and then thin slices of canes were added. The surface was then lightly pressed with a piece of wide-meshed fabric. The frame was baked in the oven at 266°F for 30 minutes.

FLATWARE

A special luncheon, buffet, or party calls for particular attention when setting the table. The flatware may be decorated with motifs that match the tablecloth or plates. The choices for designs are endless: hearts, stars, moons, flowers, etc.
If the fabric you wish to match has a special color, mix the various clay colors together to achieve the color you want..
Your guests will certainly be amazed by the originality of the motif!
Some hints on preparing the project:

MATERIALS (FOR 5 PIECES OF FLATWARE)

METAL FLATWARE
¼ OZ.. WHITE CLAY, ⅛ OZ.. LIGHT BLUE CLAY, 2 OZ.. BLUE CLAY, CRAFT KNIFE, ROLLING PIN, BAKING EQUIPMENT

by the clay's manufacturers;
(4) insert the flatware into a preheated oven (20 minutes should be enough for a perfect result);
(5) let the objects cool without touching them.
Flatware decorated with polymer clay should be washed in warm, sudsy water. Do not place them in the dishwasher.

(1) Be careful not to let air remain between the clay and the metal base of the flatware;
(2) baking must be exactly right because if not, the object will be fragile;
(3) do not exceed the temperature indicated

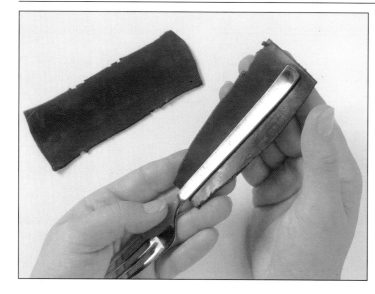

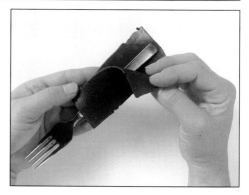

Apply a layer of blue clay to the lower part of the handle. Place another layer over the upper part.

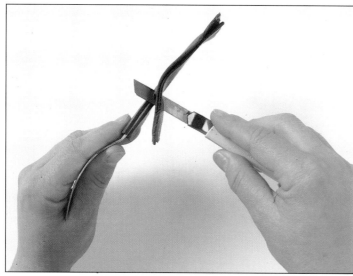

Cut off the excess clay with the craft knife. Join the two layers laterally by slightly pressing them. Create a striped cane by overlapping and alternating the white and light blue layers.

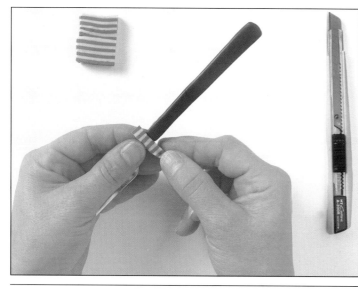

Cut a strip and apply it to the neck of the flatware piece. Shape a cane with the image of a flower. The center will be a twirl obtained by placing a blue layer over a white one, rolling them so that the blue remains on the outside. The petals are made by small white logs wrapped in blue clay.

Give this new cylinder the shape of a parallelepiped, modeling the four sides. Cut into thin slices.

Apply the canes onto the top end of the piece of flatware. Slightly press to make sure that they stick to the blue clay.

With some baby powder, smooth the surface of the piece of flatware.

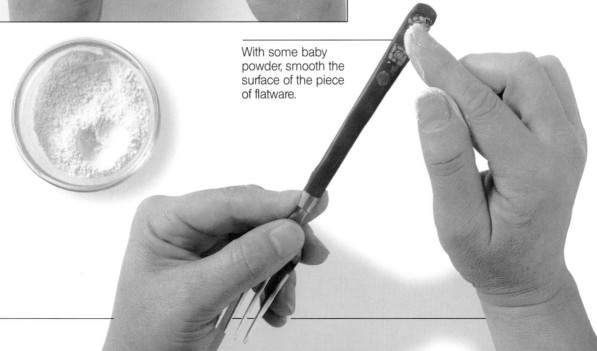

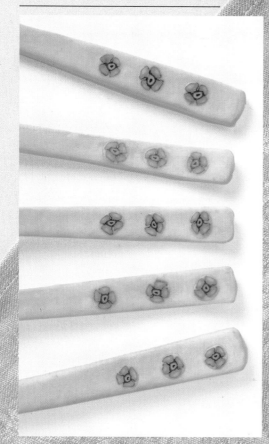

Flatware can also be decorated with other motifs. In this project, we wanted to reproduce the plate's flower motif on the flatware by using a cane depicting a four-petal flower. The petals were also made from canes with three concentric circles of different dimensions in creamy white, antique pink, and brown.

FISH

We now will concentrate on making animal shapes. The technique is the same one we have been using until now: a motif made with common geometric shapes, such as points, rectangles, squares, triangles, and lines. Two-dimensional shapes are later transformed into three-dimensional projections. A fish is the first animal we will make.

MATERIALS

WHITE, BLUE, LIGHT BLUE, GREEN, AND RED CLAY, CRAFT KNIFE, ROLLING PIN

Prepare 10 green clay rolls with a layer of blue around them. Arrange the cylinders so that you create the fish's tail. The head is made by using half of a white cylinder that has a wedge cut into the round side–the eye will later be inserted there.

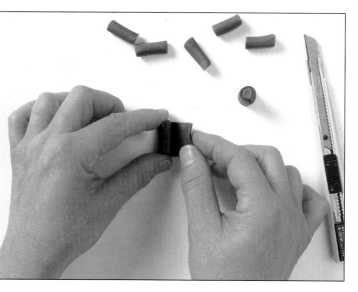

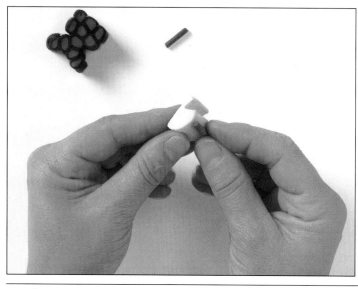

To make the mouth, insert two very thin rolls of clay. The fish's eye is nothing more than a small black cylinder with light blue clay molded into the shape of a prism. Insert it into the wedge cut.

Mold the shape as shown in the photo. Insert a small, blue roll between the red cylinders (the fish's mouth) so that they do not stick to each other while the cane is being elongated.

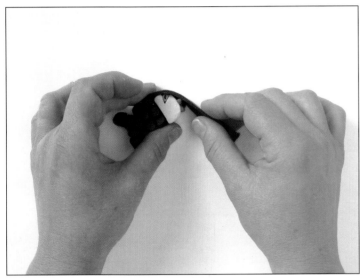

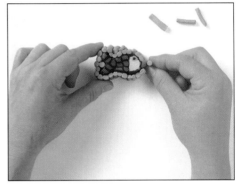

Wrap the fish's head in blue clay. Attach light blue clay sticks around the shape.

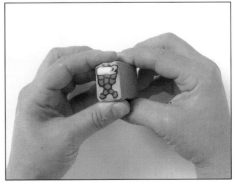

Join the motif by slightly pressing and squeezing. Give the object a parallelepiped shape while constantly reducing the cane. Once you have removed the ends, you will have the form of a fish.

BUTTONS

Making buttons is a fantastic way to spruce up your old clothing. In this project we will use a real button as the supporting structure. This simplifies the work somewhat because the button's size is already determined. You can, instead, make buttons entirely with polymer clay.

MATERIALS

A CANE WITH THE FISH MOTIF,
A BUTTON (CLAY, METAL, OR WOOD),
A SMALL AMOUNT OF YELLOW CLAY,
A PAIR OF SCISSORS, A TOOTHPICK

In our case, a transparent, plastic button was used. You do not have to unsew the buttons every time you wash the clothing. You can wash it in lukewarm water or put it in the washing machine (delicate cycle). They must never be dry cleaned or spin-dried. We chose a fish, but any design, of course, swill do.

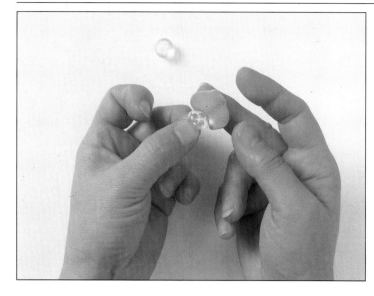

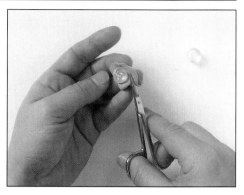

Roll a small layer of yellow clay and apply it onto the button. Cut the clay around the button with a pair of scissors, leaving a 1/8-inch border.

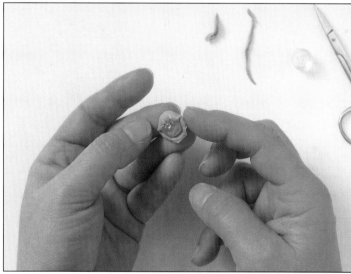

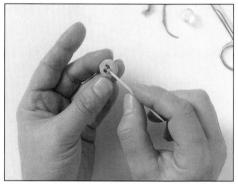

Bend the border and wrap the back part of the button. With a toothpick, pick the holes to unclog the clay.

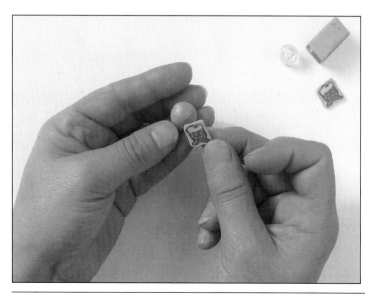

Apply a slice of cane on the facing side of the button. Smooth the surface with some baby powder. Bake the buttons for about 20 minutes at a low temperature of 266°F.

LADYBUGS

According to many, the ladybug is a lovely animal that is a lucky charm.
Ladybugs can be used to decorate buttons as well as many other objects.

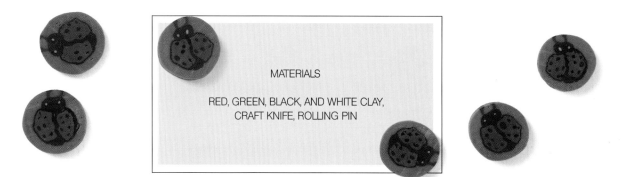

MATERIALS

RED, GREEN, BLACK, AND WHITE CLAY,
CRAFT KNIFE, ROLLING PIN

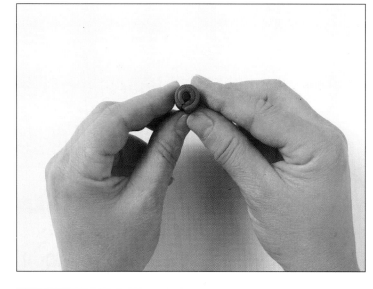

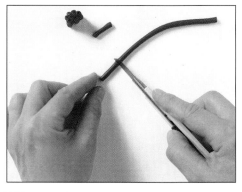

With some black clay, make a thin cord.
Wrap a thick layer of red clay around it.
Elongate the cylinder by rolling it on a flat
surface. Once you have obtained a long
and thin roll, cut it into 16 sections.

Join eight of these rolls together. Give them
a half-moon shape. Wrap them in a thin
layer of black clay. Repeat this same step
with the remaining eight. Join them together.
You will have the ladybug's body. Now give
it a cylindrical shape.

Apply a layer of black clay onto two small, white rolls. These will be the ladybug's eyes. Join these two rolls together and place them on both sides of the black partitioning line of the body, where the eyes will be placed.

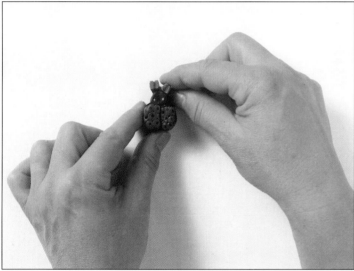

On these rolls, apply two black antennae, made by alternating a black strip with a green one. Fill in the spaces at the ladybug's side with strips of green clay until the object has a cylindrical shape.

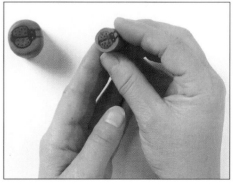

Wrap a sheet of green clay around the object. Start elongating the cane by slightly and evenly pressing on the perimeter of the cylinder. Continue elongating the cane by rolling it on a flat surface. Remove the ends and you will have a ladybug.

SNAILS

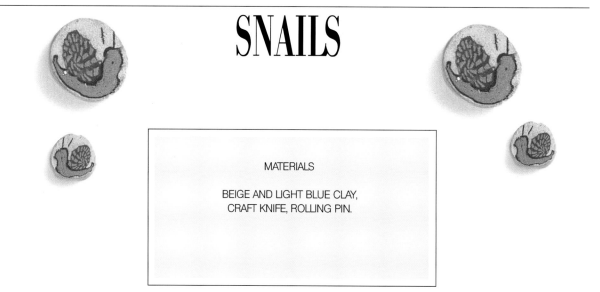

```
MATERIALS

BEIGE AND LIGHT BLUE CLAY,
CRAFT KNIFE, ROLLING PIN.
```

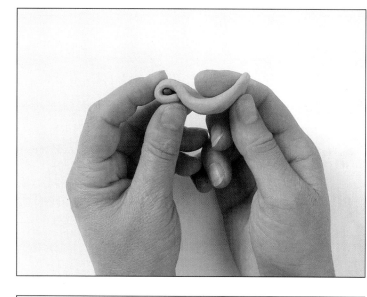

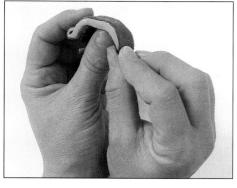

Mold a piece of beige clay. Roll one of its ends around a small, brown cylinder. Apply a thin layer of brown clay around it.

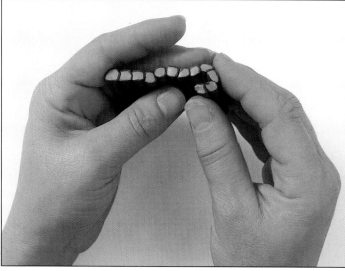

Roll together a series of beige rolls with a thin layer of brown clay around them. This will be the snail's shell.

Apply a sheet of light blue clay. Join the various parts together and add the snail's antennae, which you will have already made by alternating a brown strip with a light blue strip.

Wrap light blue clay around the entire object until it has a cylindrical shape. Begin elongating the cylinder by lightly and evenly pressing on its perimeter. Continue to elongate the "sausage" by rolling it on a flat surface. The sections of the cane can be used to cover buttons and a variety of other objects.

BUTTERFLIES

Keep in mind that you must duplicate the canes; that is,
repeat the operation until the shape is completed.

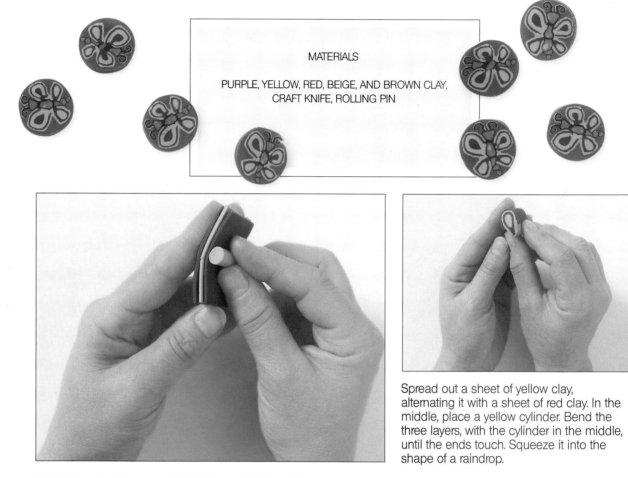

MATERIALS

PURPLE, YELLOW, RED, BEIGE, AND BROWN CLAY,
CRAFT KNIFE, ROLLING PIN

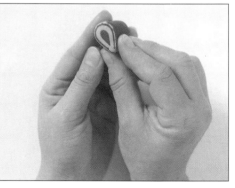

Spread out a sheet of yellow clay,
alternating it with a sheet of red clay. In the
middle, place a yellow cylinder. Bend the
three layers, with the cylinder in the middle,
until the ends touch. Squeeze it into the
shape of a raindrop.

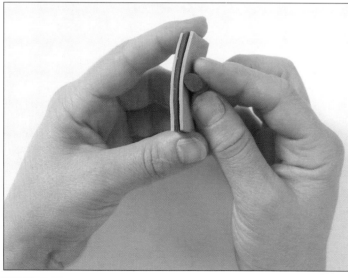

Repeat this step but this time with two
layers of red clay and one layer of yellow.
Squeeze and give it the shape of a raindrop
as well.

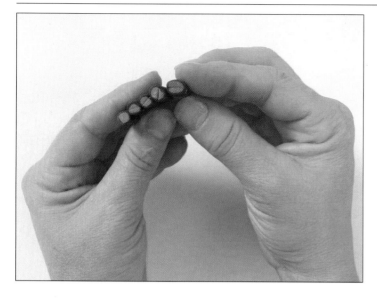

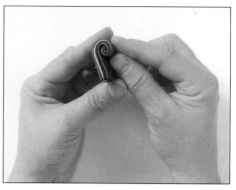

Wrap five logs of increasing size with brown clay and join them together, from the smallest to the biggest. These will be the body and head of the butterfly. Roll four sheets of clay in this order: purple, blue, yellow, and purple–this will be the butterfly's antennae.

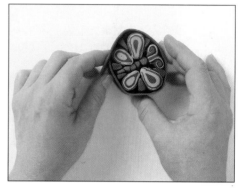

Create the shape on your worktable. Start to fill in the empty spaces with "sausages" and other geometric forms of purple-colored clay until the whole object has a cylindrical shape. Apply a strip of purple clay around the entire object.

As you did for all the other shapes created up until now, start to elongate the cane with your hands. Continue to do so by rolling the object on a flat surface. The sections of this cane were used to decorate the cups and teapot in the next project.

TEA SET WITH BUTTERFLIES

This tea set has been decorated with a butterfly design. Besides using a cane with a butterfly motif to create this, make a cane with the twirl motif by rolling two yellow and violet overlapped sheets. Apply a strip of violet clay around the rim of the cup and insert thin canes with the butterfly figure between two rows of decorations that have the twirl motif. To decorate the handle, spread a layer of violet clay completely over it. Cut a series of thin canes with the twirl motif and apply them, pressing slightly. A thin strip of clay is placed around the rim of the saucer

MATERIALS

A TEA POT, 2 TEA CUPS AND SAUCERS,
4 OZ. OF VIOLET CLAY,
¼ OZ. OF RED CLAY, ¼ OZ. OF YELLOW CLAY,
⅛ OZ. OF BEIGE CLAY, ⅛ OZ. OF BROWN CLAY, CRAFT
KNIFE, ROLLING PIN

and is then decorated with the twirl motif. To obtain good results, remember to avoid leaving air between the clay and the china, ceramics, glass, or other material. The objects are placed into a preheated oven (266°F) and baked for 20 minutes. Turn off the heat and let them cool in the oven. Baking must be exact; if it is not cooked properly, the objects will become fragile.
Tea sets decorated with polymer clay can be washed in warm, soapy water. Do not put them in the dishwasher.

FACES

To make faces, we must conquer the complex construction of a cane. The cane is rather like a puzzle.

The height of the cane can be 1 inch. When you have acquired a certain skill in lengthening and thinning canes, you can work with a height of ¾ inch.

For the first step in lengthening, the diameter of the finished cylinder must not be bigger than 1½ inches; otherwise, it will be difficult to work with. To make things easier, we have used medium-sized compositions, but the result is excellent if you work with smaller amounts of clay–there is less waste and the figure is more precise.

MATERIALS

BEIGE, RED, LIGHT BLUE, WHITE, BLACK, AND BROWN CLAY, CRAFT KNIFE, BAKING EQUIPMENT

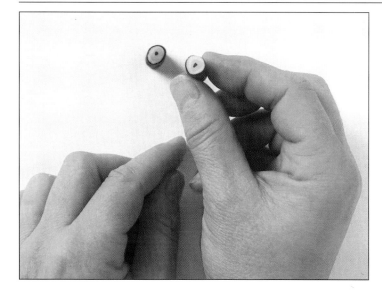

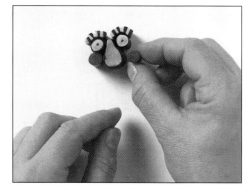

Use two small canes made up of a black stick that is in a light blue, white, and thin, black layer. These are the eyes. For the eyelashes use a thin slice of striped cane (black and white). Make sure that the lines are perpendicular.

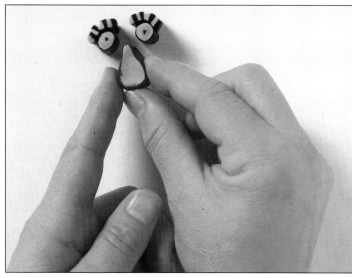

The nose is made with a prism that is wrapped on the sides with a thin, brown layer and rounded at the top. Insert this between the two eyes. Make two red cheeks with two small stubs.

With a flesh-colored layer, separate the area of the nose and cheeks from the mouth, which is colored red.
Make the chin by using another flesh-colored layer.

With small clay strips, fill in the cavities between the eyes and above the cheeks. Surround the face with a last strip.

Lengthen it, as you have done with all of the cylindrical canes. As the cylinder becomes smaller, there will be many different-sized canes. Add the hair at the end. Vary the hair style so that you have many different looking figures.

Make multicolored rings by inserting canes with twirls. Big faces, small faces with curls, faces with spiked hair (obtained with a series of strips), or bald heads—these all can decorate knobs, buttons, or whatever else comes to your mind.

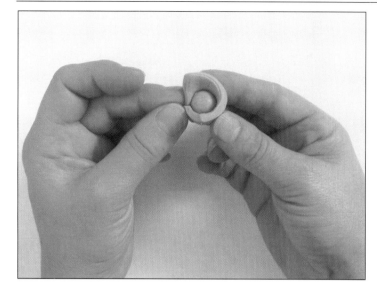

KNOBS

Roll out a small layer of light beige clay and wrap it around the knob.

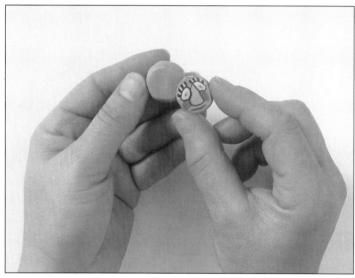

Cut a section of the cane with the face motif. Apply it to the knob that you just covered.

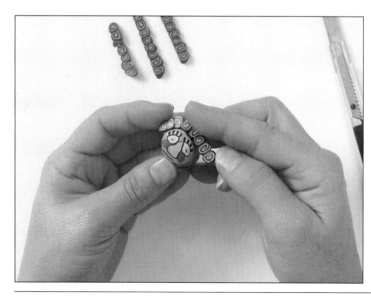

Attach a series of canes with the twirl or stripe motif to create the hair.

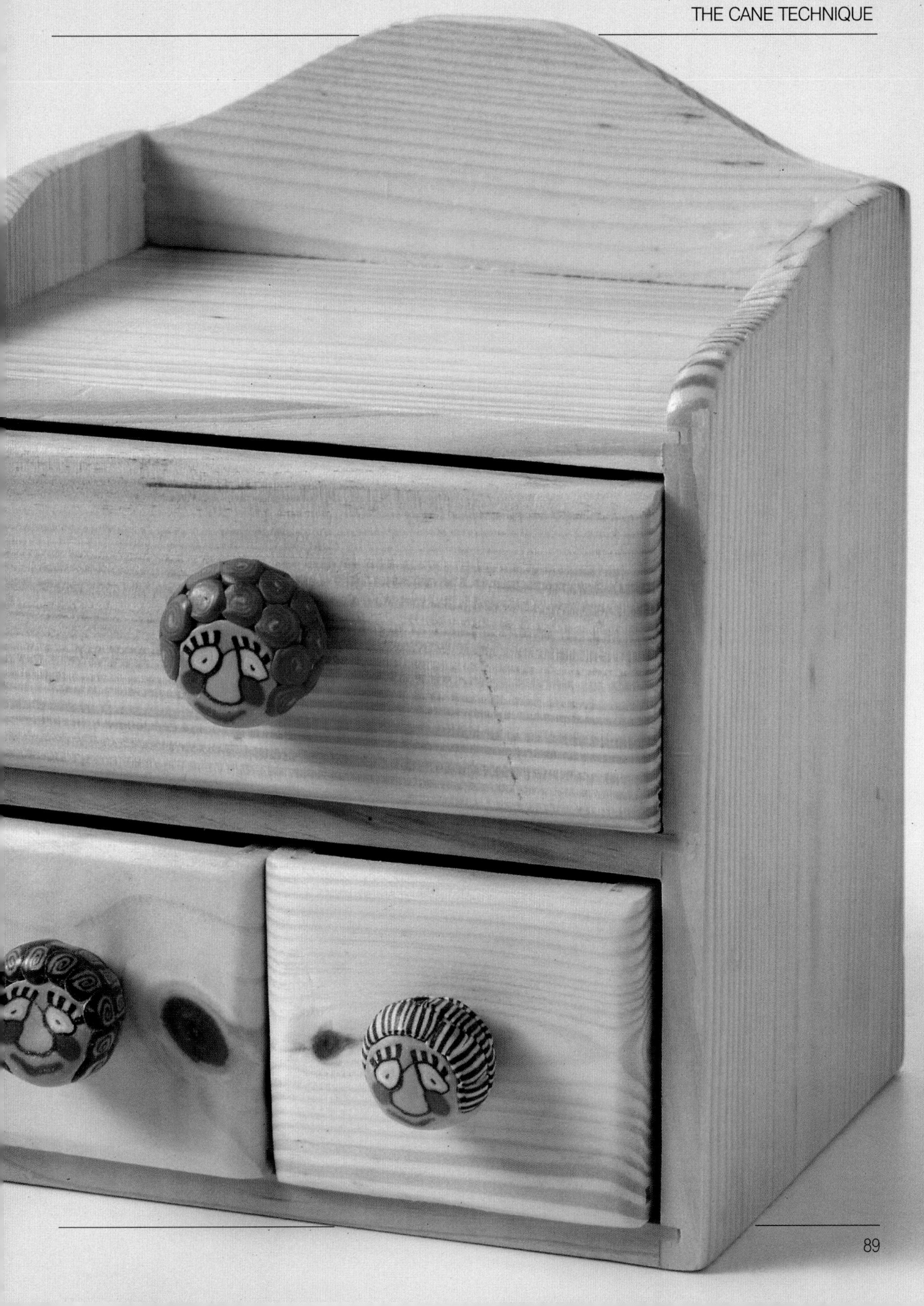

DECORATED BASKETS

To decorate these wicker baskets, we used a complex cane with a combination of different, but simple, canes that were joined together. The next project in the following pages is the first step toward making

MATERIALS

WICKER BASKET, 4 MACARONI,
WHITE TWINE (20 IN.), BLUE CLAY (1 OZ.)
TO MAKE A CANE WITH A HEART MOTIF:
PINK CLAY (⅛ OZ.), WHITE CLAY (⅛ OZ.)
TO MAKE A CANE WITH THE TWIRL MOTIF: TRANSPARENT
CLAY (¼ OZ.), BLUE CLAY (¼ OZ.),
BAKING EQUIPMENT

a complex figure. You can experiment and obtain other complex canes by joining together the leftovers from other projects. In this way you can create amusing images similar to patchwork.

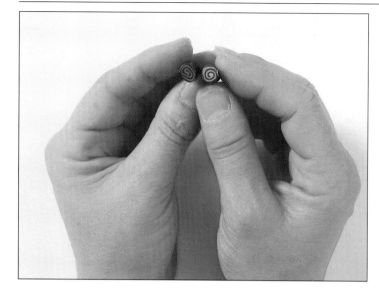

Create a cane with the twirl motif and divide it into various "sausages."

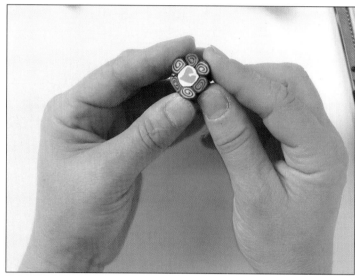

Make a cane with the heart motif and attach around it short logs with the twirl motif. Apply a layer of blue clay and place two macaroni on it. Wrap the clay with the blue sheet of clay.

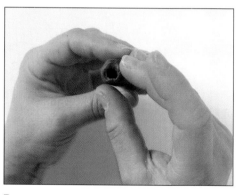

Remove any excess clay. Trim both ends to hide the clay, but leave the hole open.

Cut slices of complex cane and apply them onto the middle of the handle. On the rim of the handle, alternate decorations with the heart and twirl motifs. Put both handles into the oven and bake at 266°F for 30 minutes.

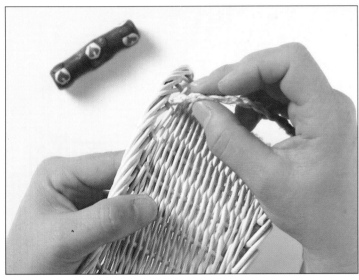

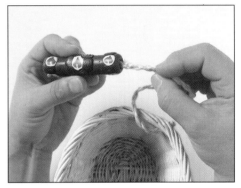

Create some space in-between the interlacing of the wicker basket since you will need to string the thread through it. Thread the string inside the handle and then reinsert the string between the wicker interlacing.

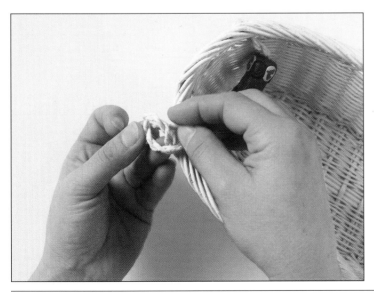

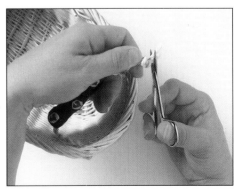

After you have calculated the desired length, tie a knot at both ends of the string. Cut off any excess string.

MIXED TECHNIQUES

JADE

The color of Chinese jade is transparent green. If you observe this stone carefully, you will see soft, white dots scattered on its surface. By following the instructions, you will be able to obtain a Chinese jade effect. It is important to use pigment-free clay in order to give the object that luminosity that is typical of hard stones. To imitate jade, I used yellow, light blue, and white translucent clay. The dosage: 3 white, 1 light blue, and 1 yellow.

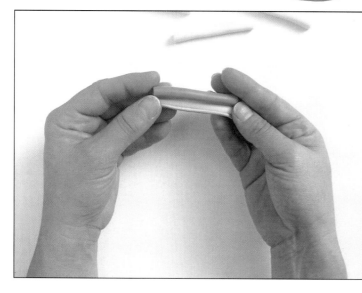

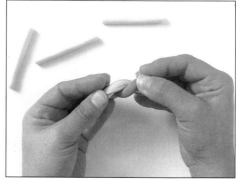

Take some yellow and light blue logs and twist them around each other, inserting between them a small white log.

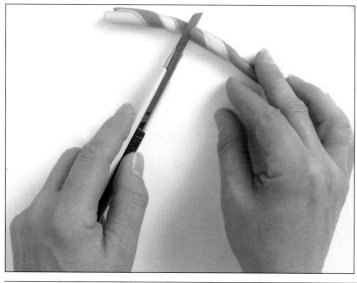

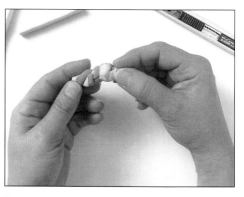

Elongate and cut into two sections. Twist the two segments together. Repeat this operation two more times. You will have a green cylinder.

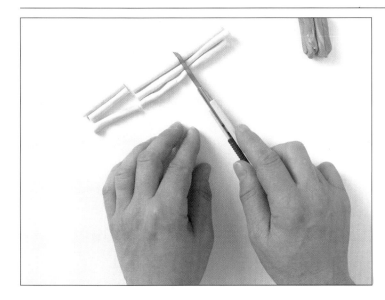

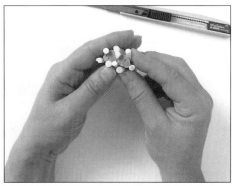

Make lots of thin logs with the white clay. Place the logs around the green cylinder.

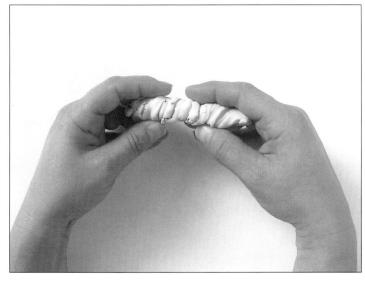

Twist everything together. Cut in half and then join the two parts together. Elongate and twist once more.

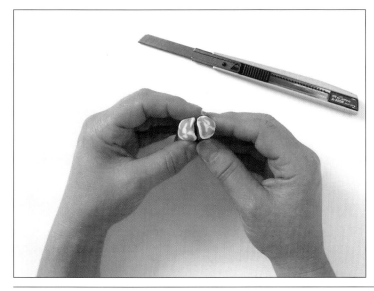

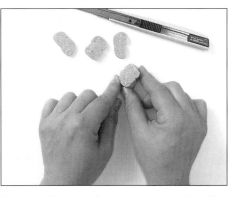

Repeat this operation many times–this will create the jade effect with small white dots scattered in the green background. Cut some sections and then apply them onto the surface.

CORAL NECKLACE

Real coral necklaces are expensive. With a small amount of clay, you can create one very similar to a real necklace. As is widely known, wax melts when heated.
By inserting pieces of wax pencils into the clay when baking, they melt and make holes in the polymer clay that are colored

> MATERIALS
>
> CORAL CLAY, WAX PENCILS IN A SIMILAR, BUT DARKER, SHADE THAN THE CLAY

by the pencil's pigment. Use a little bit of wax because real corrals usually only have a few holes on their surface. We used these properties to create beads made of artificial coral. You can make a necklace by stringing beads on a string that is the same color.

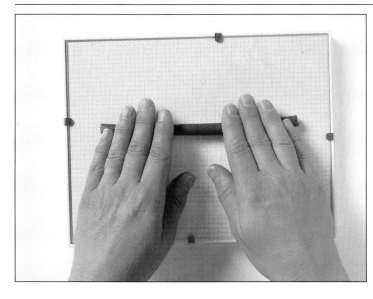

First find a glass surface. Place a sheet of graph paper (If you do not have graph paper, use a ruler.) beneath it; the surface does not have to be very big. Make a "sausage" and cut it into many identical segments.

Each segment, once rolled in the palm of your hands, will become a bead. Take a wax pencil, cut the wax into many tiny pieces, and roll the beads over them so that they remain on the surface.

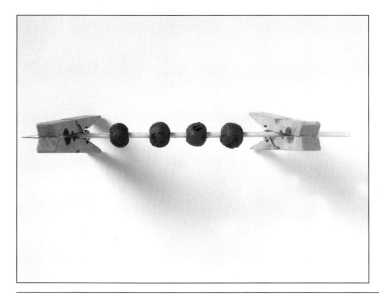

Make holes in the beads with a wooden skewer. Put the beads onto the skewer and use two pegs to support it. Place them into the oven and bake for 30 minutes at 266°F. Place a piece of cardboard on your worktable to prevent the wax from dripping onto the surface and dirtying it. (Don't worry; cardboard never burns if baked at temperatures as low as those used to bake polymer clay.)

MARBLING

To obtain the chromatic effect of marble, various colors must be mixed together without, however, being completely amalgamated. Haphazard streaks are created by streamlining rolls of various diameters and mixing them in a disorderly manner.

MATERIALS

AN EGG, MARBLED CLAY, ROLLING PIN, SKEWER, PEGS, PAIR OF SCISSORS, BABY POWDER, PAPER TAPE, SHOE POLISH

Us your left-overs from other projects to spread out a thin surface of multicol red stripes.
The resulting layer is ideal for coating eggs. Working with eggs requires extreme care, but the end result is a beautiful light, unbreakable egg.

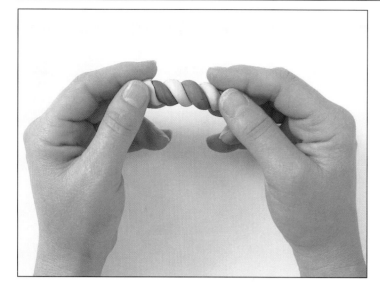

To obtain an effect of linear shapes in yellow and green, form two cylinders of yellow and light blue clay respectively. Twist them around each other. Roll out and spread the cylinder on your worktable.

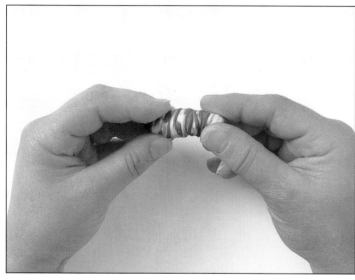

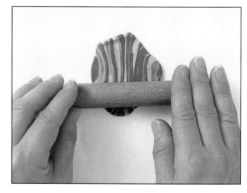

Roll the clay and twirl it around again. Flatten it once more and lengthen with a rolling pin. Roll over the new layer once more.

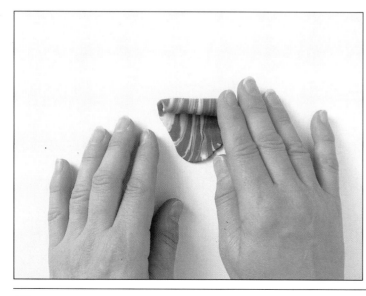

Roll once again, flatten, and spread as in the previous steps. The blue will have amalgamated with the yellow in certain points, creating a green grain, but there will also be strips of a more yellowish color.

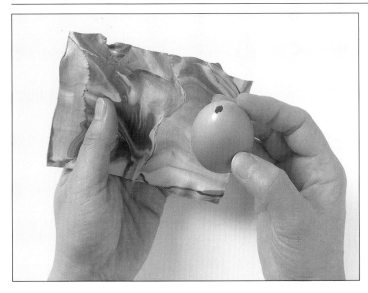

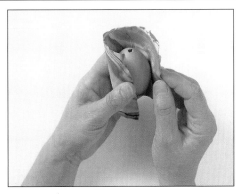

Empty, rinse, and dry the egg. Wrap it in a layer of marbled clay.

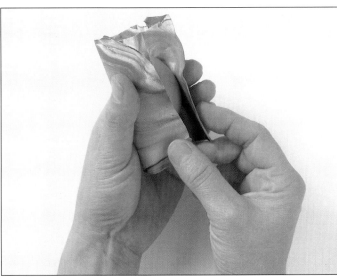

Press the clay onto the surface of the egg and onto its two ends, leaving three folds free that resemble bird wings.

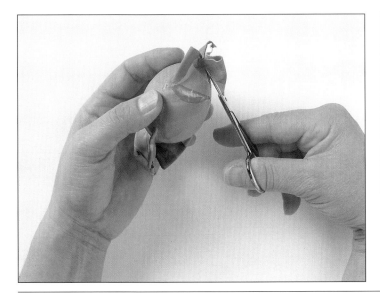

Cut the wings with scissors. With your index finger, mold any points that remained open after cutting.

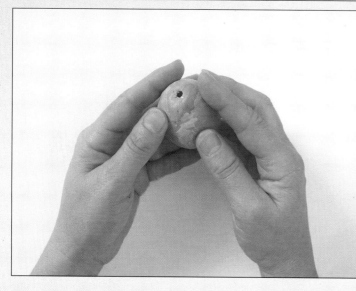

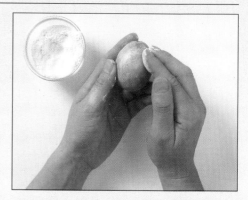

Leave the two holes in the egg uncovered. Spread baby powder onto the outside of the egg. Check to make sure that the clay has stuck to the egg and that there are no air bubbles anywhere.

Stick a skewer through the holes. Use clothespins as supports during baking. Bake for 30 minutes in an oven at 266°F.

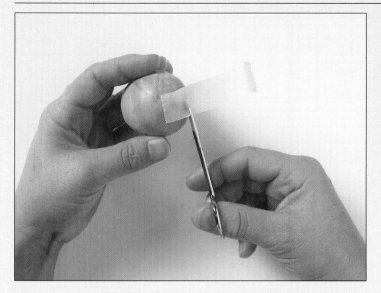

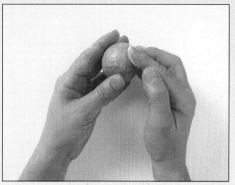

When the egg has cooled, cover the two folds with a piece of paper tape–it will act as a shield when you apply the final sheet of clay.

Cover the paper tape with clay and rub some more baby powder on it. Place the egg once more in the oven on a smooth surface. After about 15 minutes, take it out and let it cool. Polish the surface with a polishing cloth.

DABBED SURFACES

Rough surfaces not only have a different sensation to the touch, but also reflect light differently than smooth surfaces. They also hide small defects in materials. To apply a grain on material is an easy procedure, which can also be applied to other parts of the work. One of the most frequently occurring problems that happens when a surface is being covered in clay is the appearance of small air bubbles after baking. Even if these defects are minimal, they can be noticed at first glance. Dabbing the surface with a cloth transforms a smooth surface into a rough one.

A VANITY SET

Rose and light blue are very suitable for a bathroom. Because polymer clay is waterproof and has a high resistance, objects created with it can be washed.

The brush and the structure for the mirror were bought at a cheap store. They are made of wood.

The mirror has the body of a brush as its base. The glass was cut to measure it. The comb is made of plastic and must, therefore, be baked between 212 to 230°F (212°F is advised). Let it cool in the oven.

It may seem strange that plastic objects can be put in the oven, but many types can bear the heat. Some plastics soften; don't worry. Just let them cool in the oven. Regardless, I suggest a trial run by placing the object in the oven without decoration for about 10 minutes at 212 to 230°F.

MATERIALS

COMB, BRUSH, THE BODY OF ANOTHER BRUSH,
OVAL MIRROR CUT TO SIZE,
PINK CLAY (4 OZ.), LIGHT BLUE CLAY (1 OZ.),
ROLLING PIN, CRAFT KNIFE, GLUE

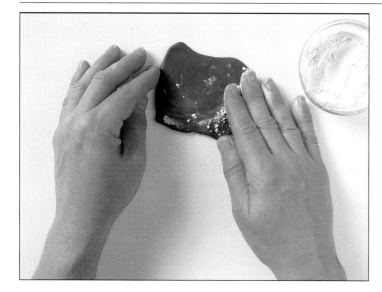

Cover the surface with baby powder. Place a wide-meshed piece of cloth over the clay and pass the rolling pin over it. Press so that you leave the mark of the fabric on the surface.

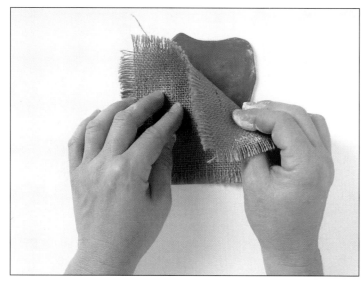

Remove the fabric, which will come away easily from the clay thanks to the baby powder. You can now see the grain of the fabric reproduced on the surface.

If the object you are working on is not flat, like the previous example, it is a good idea to make a dabber. Make a small tinfoil ball and cover it with a piece of wide-meshed fabric. You can now apply the imprint on any curved surface.

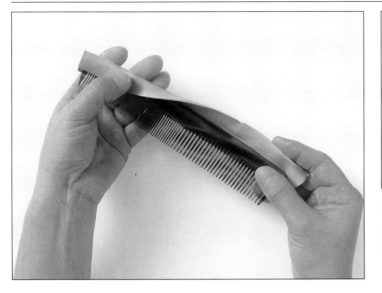

Prepare a sheet of clay. Wrap the sheet around the top part of the comb. Give the clay the shape of the comb. Cut off any excess clay at the two ends with a craft knife.

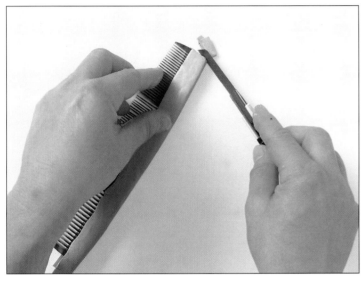

Remove any excess clay and trim the edges. Apply the canes, starting with the twirl motif at the center of the comb.

Continue to decorate with canes with the stripe motif. Dab the surface.

Remove the inner part of the brush. Spread on a thin layer of pink clay. Cut out the shape of the brush, leaving a ¼-inch border. Repeat this operation for the top part Cut the inside oval, leaving a border.

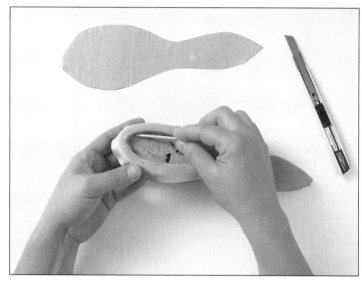

With a toothpick, tuck in the internal rim. Apply the clay to the bottom part of the brush's body and unite the borders.

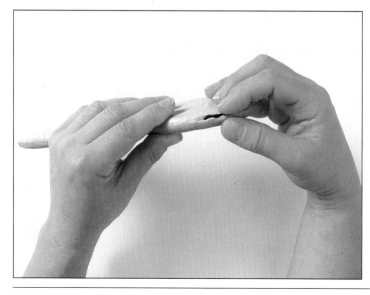

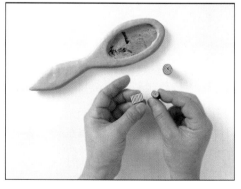

Create a cane with the stripe motif. Alternately overlap pink and blue clay and one cane with the twirl motif. Roll two sheets of clay made with the same colors that you previously used.

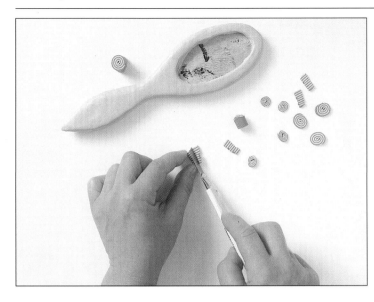

After having cut the slices, apply them to the base, stongly pressing them to stick on the surface.

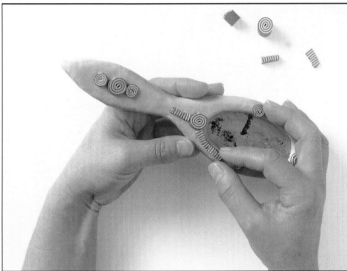

Continue the operation until you have completed the decoration. Dab the entire surface with a wide-meshed cloth. Bake in the oven for 30 minutes at 266°F. Let it cool.

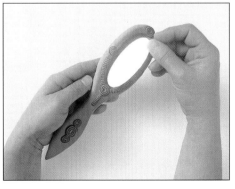

Apply the glue and insert the mirror. Follow the same instructions for the mirror for the brush. (When you tuck in the borders, leave enough space to reinsert the sponge with the bristles once its base is baked.)

GLITTER

CHRISTMAS DECORATIONS

As I have already mentioned, it is very important to have a clean worktable because all types of dust and dirt remain attached to polymer clay. With this in mind, I decided to make a project ignoring this rule— Christmas balls covered in glitter! Glitter can easily incorporated into polymer clay.

> **MATERIALS**
>
> ¼ OZ. OF BLUE CLAY, ⅛ OZ. OF WHITE CLAY, STAR-SHAPED CUTTER, THIN WIRE, PLIERS, CRAFT KNIFE, TINFOIL, GLITTER.

The surface becomes shiny and sparkles, wich is perfect for Christmas decorations. All types and colors of glitter are available. Always remember that the color of the finished object does not only depend on the color of the chosen clay, but also on the glitter. Use these small particles very carefully to avoid finding them scattered all over your house.

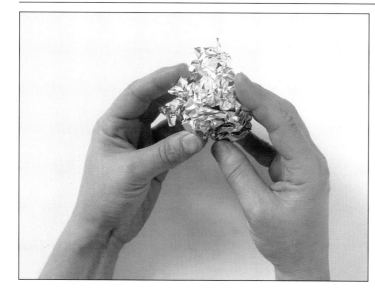

Crumple some tinfoil into a ball. The balls must not be too compact; otherwise, you will have problems inserting the hook to hang the ball.

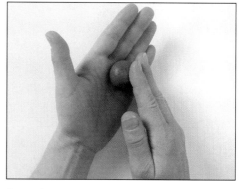

Spread out a sheet of clay. Wrap the clay around the ball. Smooth it in the palm of your hands.

Flatten some white clay and, with a star-shaped cutter, cut out a sufficient amount of stars to apply on the ball. Slightly press for them to adhere to the surface.

Dip your finger into the glitter and distribute it on the surface of the ball.

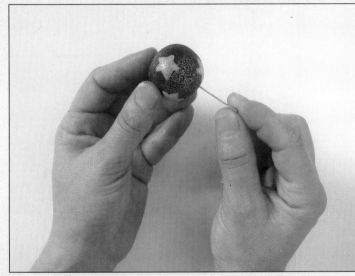

Make a hole in the ball with a skewer and, with a pair of pliers, insert a piece of thin wire. Mold it into the shape of a ring. Trim the hole that you have just made. Put the ball into the oven at 266°F and bake for approximately 30 minutes.

WITH GOLD LEAF

Golf leaf (a very thin gold foil that is available in craft stores and some hardware stores) has always been used to decorate different types of materials.

They come in very thin sheets of paste in the following colors: gold, silver, and copper.

Gold leaf must be handled very carefully because

a slight movement of air can move them. Clay coated in gold leaf can be used to make an endless variety of projects. In this project, the pen was decorated first while the base was made in a second stage.

The objects, once completed, are baked at a low temperature (212 to 230°F) for 20 minutes.

MATERIALS

A METAL REFILL, CARTRIDGE FOR PENS,
ABOUT 1 OZ. OF BLUE CLAY, ONE GOLD LEAF SHEET,
⅛ OZ. OF LEFTOVER CLAY, A CARDBOARD,
PASTA MACHINE OR ROLLING PIN, BAKING EQUIPMENT.

On a thin sheet of clay, place a sheet of gold leaf. Slightly press to combine the two surfaces. If you have a pasta machine handy that is used only for working with polymer clay, place it at the thickest setting and pass the two strips through.

The result will be a fragmented gold motif. You can spread the clay with a rolling pin—use a slight, uniform pressure over the entire surface in order to obtain regular fragmentation.

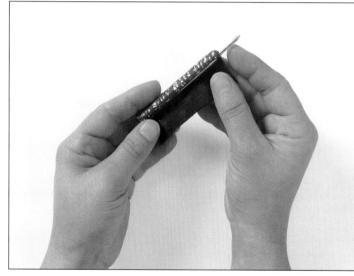

Wrap the pen's refill cartridge with the gold leaf, leaving the area around the tip free. Remove any excess clay.

You have now obtained a three-quarters covered pen. Roll the pen until the clay coats the entire surface of the refill cartridge. Make sure the lower end is thinner.

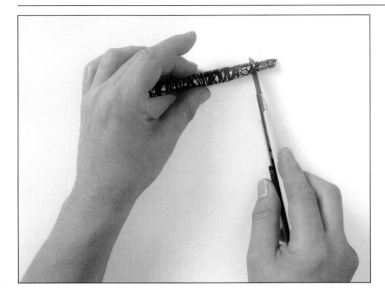

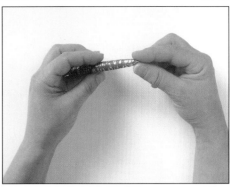

Remove any excess clay. Turn the tip around.

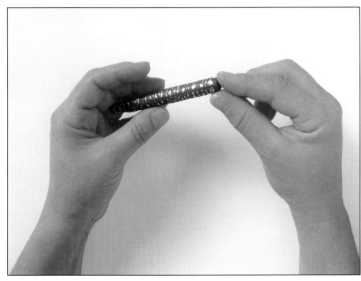

Round the top end of the pen. Apply the same gold leaf motif onto a ball made from the leftovers. This will be the pen's supporting structure.

After the work has been completed, it is now time to bake. You are probably asking yourselves whether or not the cartridge of the fountain pen will get ruined in the oven. The answer is that nothing will happen if the temperature doesn't exceed 230°F and if the object is placed in a cold oven.
Fold a piece of cardboard as shown in the photo and place the pen on one of the folds. Protected by the cardboard, polymer clay will not be deformed during baking. Bake the pen for 20 minutes. If the temperature is higher, you risk having a pen that doesn't write!

REPRODUCING AN IMAGE

Transposing an image onto paper is another effect you can obtain using polymer clay. The image, once transposed on the clay, will have a mirror-like effect.

MATERIALS

COLORED CHALK, WHITE CLAY (ABOUT ½ OZ.), STENCIL, CRAFT KNIFE, ROLLING PIN, GLUE, A SHEET OF DRAWING PAPER, PHOTO ALBUM, BAKING EQUIPMENT

Images created with chalk adhere the best to polymer clay. Chalk powder unites to clay and, after baking, the color becomes permanent.

Take your stencil and place it onto a sheet of drawing paper. Draw the shape with colored chalk; make sure that its surface is well covered.

Prepare a sheet of clay that can hold the image.

Place the picture onto the clay, slightly pressing the entire surface. The picture will be impressed onto the clay. Put it into the oven for 15 minutes at 266°F.

Once it cools, spread some glue onto the back of the clay and attach it to the album.

CLAY STAMPS

Polymer clay can make all kinds of details. Thanks to this characteristic, it can be used to make a mold exactly like the original model. The clay stamp technique has endless applications. A cameo, a coin, and any part of a wide surface can be duplicated. You can create a motif and then obtain endless copies of it through this technique. If you would rather create the object yourself, you must first design and make it with the clay and, when completed, place it in the oven at the indicated temperature. After baking, let it cool. From these molds, even the slightest details may be reproduced, which can then be printed on raw clay. To make a clay stamp, soften the clay. The clay must be able to take on the shape of the object to reproduce its details.

To detach it from the original mold, it is necessary to use baby powder. Should you want to reproduce the relief of an object, for example a cameo or a motif in wood, place everything into the oven, after having sprinkled the surface to be copied with

> MATERIALS
>
> FLOWERPOT, WHITE CLAY (¼ OZ), RED CLAY (1 ½ OZ).
> A MOLD WITH A FLOWER MOTIF, SCISSORS,
> ROLLING PIN, PAINTBRUSH, BABY POWDER, CRAFT KNIFE,
> BAKING EQUIPMENT

baby powder and covering it completely with some clay. In this way, when the heat of the oven softens the clay, you do not risk your creation.

Some polymer clays, after baking, are more flexible than others and it is, therefore, advisable to use the appropriate one to make the clay stamps. We will use a flower motif as an example. Naturally, you can create other motifs to reproduce.

FLOWERPOTS

In this project we have used actual flowers to decorate the rim of a flowerpot. This pot can be placed outdoors because polymer clay is not affected by rain or sun. The mold with the flower motif was made by arranging small balls on a plane of clay. One of these balls was placed in the middle and the remaining six were arranged all around it. With a toothpick, holes were made on the central part and rays were traced around this part to create small, decorative petals.

MAKING THE CLAY STAMP MOLD

Spread out a sheet of clay and make six small balls. Apply one of them to the clay—this will be the center of the flower. Distribute the remaining ones around it, as if they were petals.

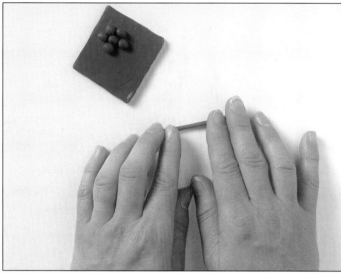

Roll a small quantity of clay, enough to make a cord, and attach it (this will be the flower's stem). Complete the flower with the leaves, placing them at the sides of the stem.

With a toothpick, make a series of holes in the middle part of the flower. Around the center, on the petals, make some lines similar to sun rays.
Once completed, place it into the oven and bake for 20 minutes at 266°F.

Let cool. Then, with a brush, sprinkle the surface with baby powder so that everything is covered in white. With some clay, make a round shape. Squeeze it onto the mold until every space is covered.

Place the baked mold and the unbaked clay shape into the oven for 20 minutes at 266°F. Let cool. Remove the stamp. You will see that every single detail has been reproduced.

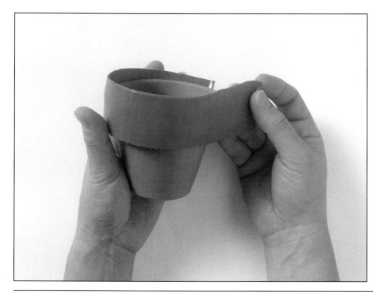

USING THE CLAY STAMP MOLD

Cut a strip of clay as long as the flowerpot's rim and a little wider than its frame.
Press it onto the rim and be sure it adheres well.

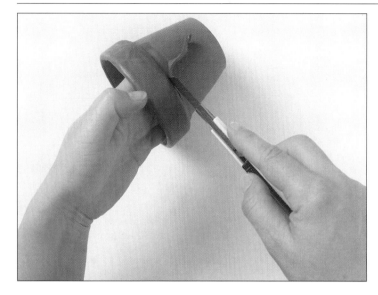

With a craft knife, remove any excess clay. Eliminate from the inside rim any excess clay while still leaving some tucked in.

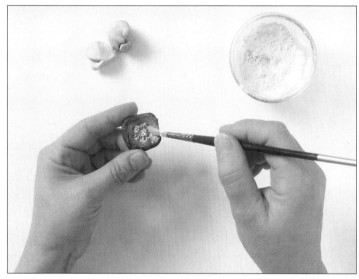

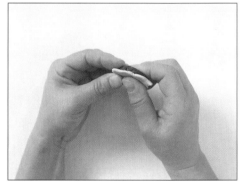

Using a paintbrush, sprinkle the mold with baby powder. Press some white clay into the mold.

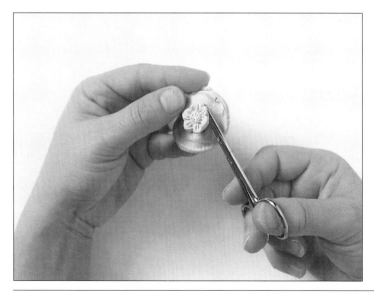

Detach the clay and cut the outline of the flower with a pair of scissors. Create seven flowers to apply around the flowerpot. Apply the molded shapes onto the rim and, with the top part of the paintbrush, make the clay adhere to the surface.

YELLOW FRAME

The frame used in this project can hold either a mirror or a photograph. The clay stamp mold for the frame was made from the edge of a carved wooden box. You could reproduce motifs from old frames so that you have "L"-shaped mold. The "L"-shape was chosen because it can be applied on both the long and short sides of the frame. It also gives you the possibility to choose the place that must be interrupted to join the two sections.

The drawing must have a certain flow, but with a little

MATERIALS

A 4 X 5-IN. WOODEN FRAME, GOLD CLAY (3 OZ.),
AN "L"-SHAPED CLAY STAMP, BABY POWDER, ROLLING PIN,
PAINTBRUSH, CRAFT KNIFE,
BAKING EQUIPMENT

skill, you can hide the inconsistencies, which sometimes arise from joining two sections together. This project requires that you pay special attention when applying the clay.

The clay must adhere well to the wooden support and must be played with for a long time. This is why I advise you to complete the frame it two stages:

(1) Cover the frame with a thin sheet of clay.
(2) Apply the molded shapes onto a previously worked base.

Make a thin sheet of gold clay. Cut into four trapezoids and apply them to the frame. Tuck in all the edges.

Finish off the grooves and junctures with the tip of a paintbrush. With some soft clay, mold a sheet into the shape of an "L". The clay used to reproduce the motif must be thin.

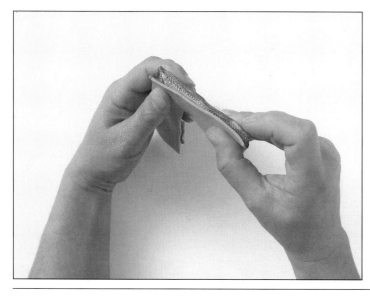

Apply the sheet of clay over the mold and press the entire surface for a while so that the clay covers the entire mold. Place the molded shape onto the frame covered in clay.

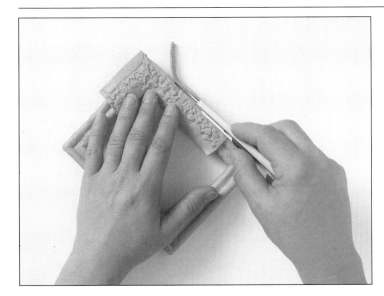

With a craft knife, cut away the protruding edges. Finish and attach the shapes with the tip of the paintbrush's handle.

Making sure not to squash the previous applications, complete the decoration of the frame and cut away any excess clay. Again, use the tip of the paintbrush's handle to give the finishing touches to the juncture points of the motif.

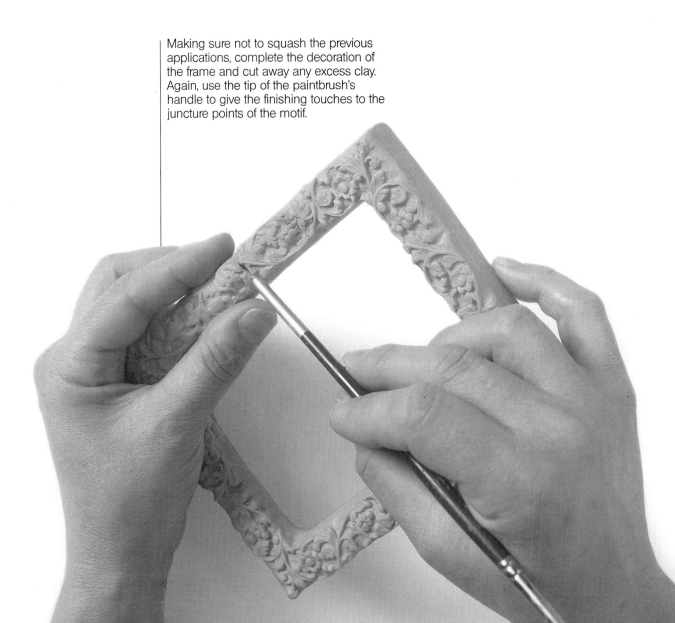

ENGRAVING

CUTTING TECHNIQUE
Polymer clay can be cut and engraved.
In the following two projects we will use cookie cutters, which can usually be found in kitchenware stores.
The shapes are engraved onto a thin surface.
The engraved part of the clay is removed and you can choose whether or not to leave the motif bare or to replace it with another sheet of a different-colored clay.

MATERIALS

SMALL COOKIE CUTTERS, SMALL AMOUNTS OF RED, PINK, YELLOW, AND WHITE TRANSPARENT CLAY, LIGHT BLUE CLAY (¼ OZ.), GREEN CLAY (2¾ OZ.), SCISSORS, PENCIL, ERASER, A PIECE OF GLASS AS BIG AS THE SHAPE OF THE LAMP, CRAFT KNIFE, DOUBLE-SIDED ADHESIVE TAPE, METAL STRUCTURE FOR THE ABAT-JOUR, BAKING EQUIPMENT

In the first project we filled in the empty spaces while in the second one, we kept he empty spaces bare.

LAMP
Constructing a lamp is not difficult, but it does require a lot of patience and attention.
To prevent your work from damagè, you must bake it in various stages.
Two bakings are sufficient to complete the projects.

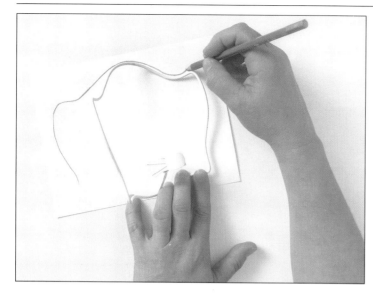

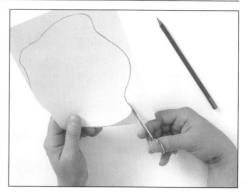

With a pencil, draw the outline of the lamp structure on a sheet of paper. Cut the shape with a pair of scissors. It will serve as a stencil to determine the outline of the lamp on the clay.

On a piece of glass, spread a thin layer of green clay so that it covers 4/5's of the height of the lamp. Make a rectangle and attach on it a strip of light blue clay. The resulting rectangle must be big enough to fit the outline of the lamp. Make sure that the two colors are well joined at all points.

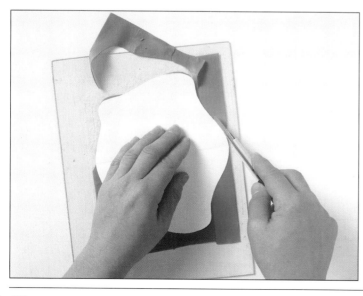

Place the stencil onto the rectangle and cut the contour of the shape. Take some cookie cutters and engrave the clay so that you obtain a regular decoration with these figures. Remove the cutouts.

With pink, red, yellow, and white clay, make the shapes to fill in the empty spaces. Fit them in. Without removing your work from the piece of glass, place it into a cool oven and bake at 266°F for 15 minutes. Let it cool in the oven.

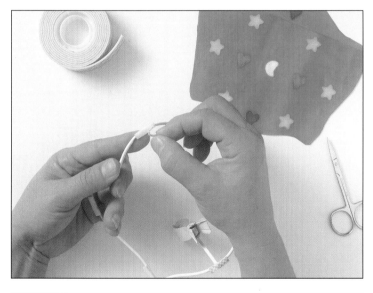

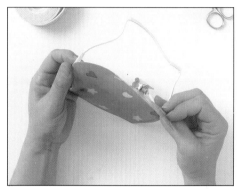

Cut small pieces of double-sided adhesive tape and place them onto the back of the metal structure. Once you have coated the edges of the shape, the tape can be removed. Remove the clay from the glass and arrange it onto the metal structure, making sure to position it properly.

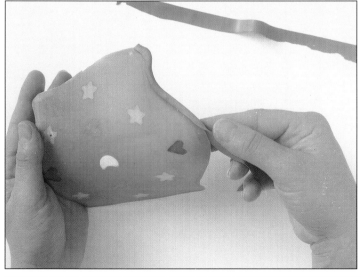

Prepare a long, thin strip of light blue clay to apply around the shape, both as a support and as a finishing touch. Remove the pieces of tape as you apply the strip of clay. At this stage the object must be baked once more. It is important that the object be placed into the oven with the front facing upward; otherwise, due to its weight, it could detach itself from the border during baking. Furthermore, if the fixture doesn't rest on a surface while in the oven, it tends to sink. This can be solved by placing a curved piece of cardboard underneath it (to act as a support) or by removing the object from the oven while it is still relatively hot and then restoring its initial shape.

INLAY

CANDLEHOLDER
Coating glass is another one of the many possible applications of polymer clay.
This next project we propose in these pages is a candleholder. We concentrated on taking advantage of the characteristics that can be obtained by reducing the material into a very thin sheet.
Furthermore, the inlay technique makes it possible to

MATERIALS

A COGNAC GLASS, COOKIE CUTTERS, LIGHT BLUE CLAY (1 ½ OZ.), ROLLING PIN, CRAFT KNIFE, BAKING EQUIPMENT

create shapes that can then be highlighted when illuminated from within.
For this project you will need a pasta machine in order to obtain a thin sheet of clay.
Given the fact that the work must be carried out in various sections, you can use a rolling pin–making sure, however, to roll the clay as much as possible.

Make thin sheets of clay and apply them onto the glass until it is completely covered. If the sheet of clay is thin enough, you only need to press slightly for it to adhere to the glass.

Once the glass has been covered completely, engrave some shapes using the cookie cutters. Remove the engraved clay so that the glass underneath is visible. Bake in the oven at 266°F for 15 minutes.

MOSAIC

Mosaics go back a long time. In ancient Mesopotamia in 3,000 BC, mosaics were used to pave the streets with stones of different colors. In ancient Rome, walls, ceilings, and floors in both public and private places were decorated with mosaics. These decorations are made with small pieces of glass or other materials that are glued onto a support. Small spaces are left between each piece, which are later filled in with cement.

The glass normally used to make mosaics is not transparent. It has, nonetheless, a glossy surface. With clay it is possible to obtain the glass effect that is typical of mosaics.

The advantage of using polymer clay is that it can be cut easily with a craft knife or a pair of scissors. The pieces can then be worked with the technique used

> MATERIALS
>
> A BOTTLE, A SHEET OF GLASS, CRAFT KNIFE (OR SCISSORS), YELLOW (⅛ OZ.), PINK (⅛ OZ.), LIGHT BLUE (¼ OZ.), AND GRAY CLAY (1 OZ.), BAKING EQUIPMENT

for traditional mosaic or can be applied, as in our project, on a soft layer of polymer clay.

For the surface to have the glossy look, use a piece of glass as a base for baking. The area in contact with the piece of glass will remain glossy even after baking.

f you would like to have a wide variety of glass pieces, you can, besides making them in different colors, cover some with gold leaf, glitter, or embossing powders.

The mosaic technique is simple. It is a meticulous job, but it will give you a great-looking result.

For the vase, we will use the polymer clay itself as a sealing agent.

We first have to make the glass pieces that, once baked, will be placed into soft clay.

They will attach during the second baking.

Roll out some pink, yellow, and light blue clay on a glass surface. Place it into the oven and bake for 15 minutes at 266°F. Let it cool. Cut the strip with a pair of scissors or a craft knife into many pieces.

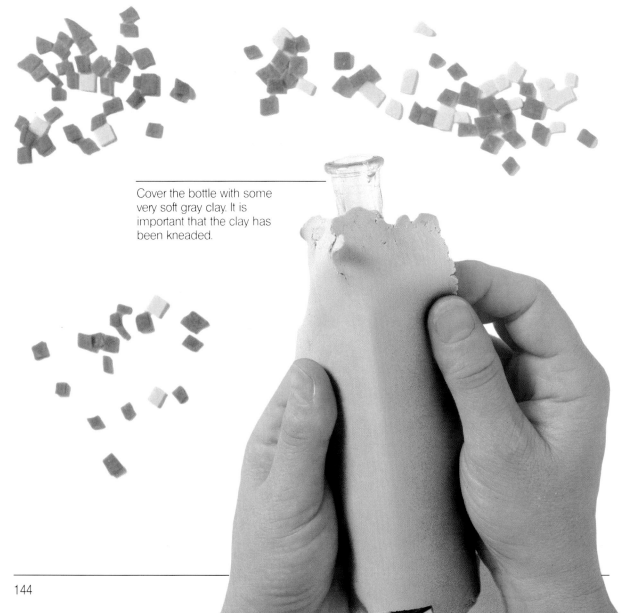

Cover the bottle with some very soft gray clay. It is important that the clay has been kneaded.

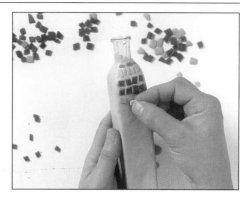

Complete the borders and start to apply the pieces of clay, leaving some space between them. Use the right amount of pressure on each piece so that it adheres well to the unbaked clay.

Continue until the whole surface is covered. Check that the pieces are well placed in the clay–gray clay must be visible all around. Place the object into the oven and bake for 30 minutes at 266°F. Let it cool.

MOKUMÉ GANE

Mokumé Gane is an old technique for working metals that originated in Japan. Various layers of different-colored metals are overlapped and given an undulating shape, which creates protruding parts. The humps are eliminated so that the underlying colored layers become visible.

MATERIALS

CLAY OF FOUR VIVID COLORS, ROLLING PIN, CRAFT KNIFE, PIECE OF CARDBOARD, A PEN TO WRITE THE GUESTS' NAMES, A TOOTHPICK., BAKING EQUIPMENT

The different streaks create very decorative, abstract motifs.

PLACE CARDS
This project is very simple, and can be made a couple of hours before your guests arrive. These cards will certainly give a very original touch to your table.

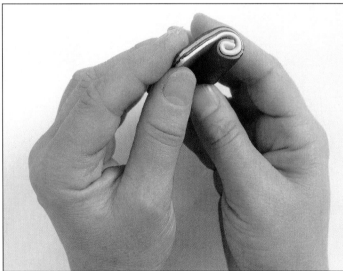

Roll four thin 2 x 1¼-inches layers of clay. Decide which of the colors you would rather have on the outside. Overlap the layers over each other. Squeeze one of the shortest sides of this four-layered plane.

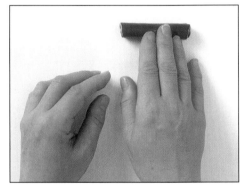

Roll, beginning from the thin side. Make sure that the color you have chosen to remain on the outside is on the outside. Roll the log until it measures 8 inches (with about ½ inch diameter).

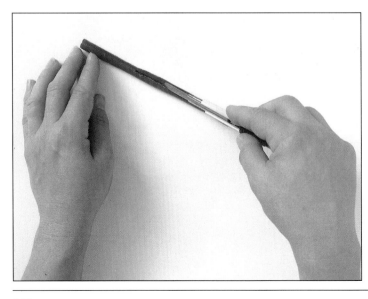

With a sharp paring knife, cut about 2 in. down the middle of this strip of clay. To the right and left of this cut, make a shallow canal with a toothpick.

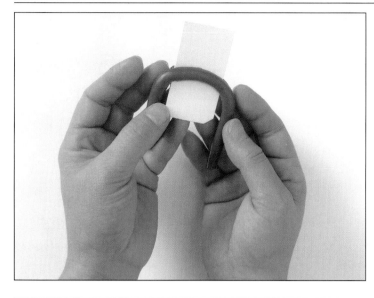

Prepare a piece of cardboard, about 1½ in. wide and 3 in. high. Insert it into the cut until you have covered ½ of its length. Fold the "sausage" so that the edges of the cardboard fit into the marked canals.

Wrap the card until the two ends touch in the center of the lower part. Join them together so that you create a pedestal for the place card. Start decorating with the Mokumé Gane technique.

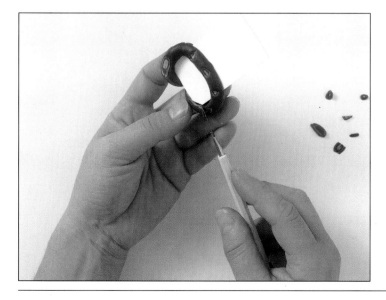

Cut small slices that will make the various layers visible.
During baking, the clay tends to soften and the object, under its weight, could end up deformed. To prevent this from happening, place a toothpick between the card and the pedestal. Place everything (the card, toothpick, and clay) into the oven for 20 minutes at 266°F.

INLAYS

The inlay technique originated in the East. The first marble inlays were discovered in Asia Minor at Alicarnasse in 350 BC. This technique is usually carried out on wood, but it can also be made with ivory, mother-of-pearl, precious stones, and other materials. The image or decoration is made with small pieces of wood or other types of materials. The inlay technique with wood or stones requires a lot of precision because every single piece must fit perfectly with the adjacent one. When using polymer clay, however, there is no risk of making mistakes.

A SPRING FLOWER
In this project we shall use polymer clays that give our work a relatively transparent effect. The inlay technique will be applied. The motif can be hung on a window.

MATERIALS

WHITE, ORANGE, YELLOW, RED, AND LIGHT BLUE TRANSPARENT CLAY (THE AMOUNTS ARE NOT INDICATED BECAUSE THEY DON'T EXCEED ⅛ OZ.), TRACING PAPER, PENCIL, TOOTHPICK, CRAFT KNIFE, ROLLING PIN, SHEET OF GLASS (4 X 6 IN.), BAKING EQUIPMENT

With a pencil and a sheet of tracing paper, copy the picture: a flower with a two-colored center, orange petals, and a green stem. Pressing slightly, pass a toothpick over the outline of the petals so that you leave a mark on the clay.

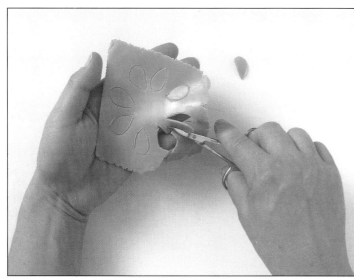

With a pair of scissors, cut the petals that are engraved on the orange clay. Place a sheet of glass onto the picture and then, on top of this, start arranging the petals in correspondence with the picture.

Regarding the central part, roll a very small amount of red clay and proceed like the petals. Place the pre-cut center over this, reproducing the original drawing. Arrange the stem and the leaves.

Once you have cut the leaves, following the same steps as those for the petals and the center of the flower, place them as depicted in the drawing under the sheet of glass. The first step of the work is now completed.
Place it into the oven for 15 minutes at 266°F and let cool.
The first half of the inlay, once baked, will not amalgamate with the added clay in the next stage. The final work will be perfect in every part. Tiny defects may occur during working. If so, just add very small amounts of clay and remodel the area.

Take the yellow clay and insert it into the center of the flower. To make sure that every piece has been correctly placed, raise the glass and check it against the light. To insert the background, fill in the spaces by stretching the clay all around the flower. You will inevitably leave some tiny spaces unfilled–don't worry! Simply add a little bit of clay and move it around a bit.

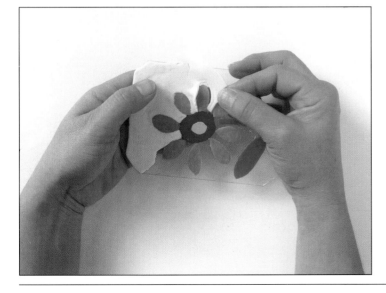

If the background is too difficult to handle, apply it in various stages.
Use a toothpick to help you unite the different areas. Once the drawing appears perfect on its surface, place it into the oven and bake for 15 minutes at 266°F.

MODELING SMALL SHAPES

A CHRISTMAS TREE UNDER THE SNOW
Having been born and raised in a hot place where snow only existed in stories, I have always appreciated those magical snow globes with snow-covered cities inside. If you one day decide to spend the winter Holidays in a warm place, take with you the next project in the following pages because there the snow is nothing but a dream.

Most objects can be made with basic forms: balls, logs, sheets, cones, cubes, etc. Our Christmas motifs are made with these simple structures.

MATERIALS

A SMALL GLASS,
WATER, CRAFT KNIFE, SCISSORS, SILICONE GLUE,
GLITTER, MOTHBALLS, WHITE (⅛ OZ.), GREEN (⅛ OZ.),
LIGHT GREEN (¼ OZ.), PINK (⅛ OZ.), RED (¼ OZ.),
PURPLE (⅛ OZ.), YELLOW (⅛ OZ.), BLUE (⅛ OZ.),
AND BROWN (⅛ OZ.) CLAY, BAKING EQUIPMENT

You must check that the dimensions of the work are right; otherwise, they will not fit into the glass.

NATIVITY
To make the characters of the Nativity, basic shapes were used, such as cones for the body, spheres for the head, and sheets of clay for the cloaks. The faces are just slices of canes with the face motif that was applied to a ball of clay.
By reducing the cane, you will obtain faces of different sizes so you can have a small face for Jesus. Instead of using a glass, the top part of a plastic bottle was used.

With a craft knife, cut a small brown cylinder to make the base of the pine tree. Stick a toothpick inside the cylinder to act as the tree's support.

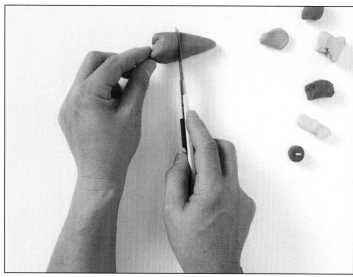

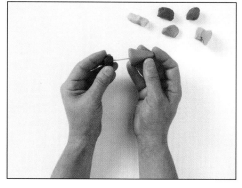

With a cone made of dark green clay, make the tree. Insert the toothpick into the cone.

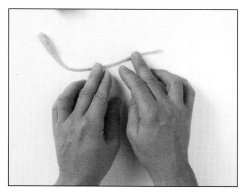

Make a small cube with some red clay, which will be one of the Christmas presents. After having made other cubes with blue, pink, and purple clay, create a very thin string with yellow clay.

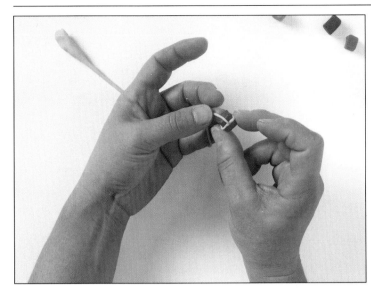

Tie the yellow string into a bow around the presents, which will be arranged around the tree. Use a toothpick to help you with the knot.

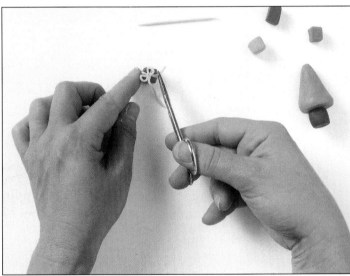

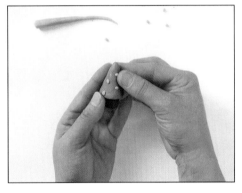

Cut the string with a pair of scissors. Apply small decorative balls onto the tree and slightly press for them to adhere.

Soften the green clay and make a ball by rolling it between the palms of your hands. Flatten the ball until it takes on the shape of a disk, which will cover the mouth of the glass.

Press a glass onto the green disk. Decorate the tree with glitter.

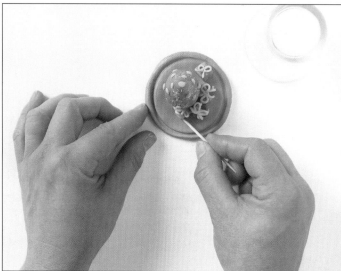

Arrange the composition on the green disk and make sure that all the pieces adhere to the base because, once completed, they will be immersed in water. With the toothpick, mark the base, which will create the effect of grass.

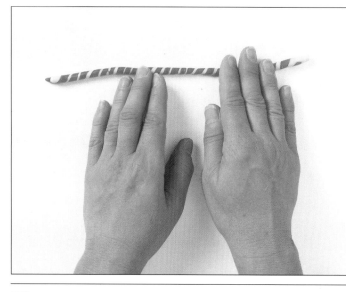

Roll two strings of red and white clay together. Elongate until it is long enough to outline the entire base. Apply it all around as a decoration.

Sprinkle the rim of the glass with baby powder. Turn it upside down onto the surface. Place the tree in a cool oven. Bring the temperature to 266°F and bake for 20 minutes.

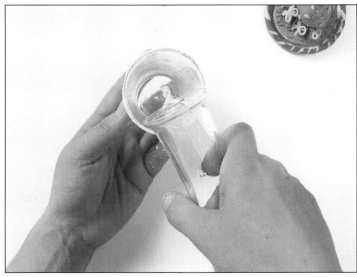

Fill the glass with water, leaving some space for the objects. Grate some mothballs and pour them into the water.

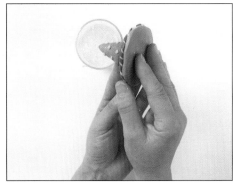

With some silicone glue, fill the canal around the composition. Close the glass containing your work. The rim of the glass must fit nicely into the canal. Let the glue dry before turning your work over.

INDEX